*Who can find a proper grave*

*for such damaged mosaics of the mind*

*where they may rest in pieces?*

LAWRENCE LANGER

Who can bring a proper grave

for such damaged mosaics of the mind

where they may rest in pieces?

LAWRENCE LANGER

# THE DREAMING WAY

*Dreamwork and Art*
*for*
*Remembering and Recovery*

PATRICIA REIS

AND

SUSAN SNOW

Chiron Publications
Wilmette, Illinois

Editing / Jane LeCompte

Book and cover design / Susan Kress Hamilton

Photography / Jay York

Printing / Penmor Lithographers, Lewiston. Maine

On the cover: *"Burial Mound"*, Monotype by Susan Snow, 30" x 40"
Collection of Charles and Linda Nichols


Art reproduced from the collections of:
Boston Public Library / *"Desert Pears," "Big Bird Shaman"*
Rosemary and David Armington / *"The Combing," "Dream Interior," "The Dancers"*
Charles Osgood / *"Spirit Bowl"*
Caryn McHose / *"The Jewel Box"*
Margaret Smalzel / *"One Who Sees"*
David Smith / *"Lizard Games"*
Patricia Reis / *"Queen of the Night"*

Copyright Acknowledgments:
Hinsey, Ellen (1996), "The Roman Arbor," *Cities of Memory*, 43-44,
Yale Series of Younger Poets, Vol. 91, Yale University Press: New Haven and London.
Langer, Lawrence (1991), *Holocaust Testimonies: The Ruins of Memory*,
Yale University Press: New Haven and London.
Oliver, Mary (1992), "White Night," *New and Selected Poems*, Beacon Press: Boston.

Library of Congress Cataloging-in-Publication Data

Reis, Patricia, 1940-
    The dreaming way : dreamwork and art for remembering and recovery /
Patricia Reis and Susan Snow.
        p. cm.
    ISBN 1-888602-11-2 (pbk.)
    1. Adult child sexual abuse victims. 2. Dreams--Therapeutic use. 3.
Art therapy. 4. Recovered memory.  I. Snow, Susan, 1954-    . II. Title.

    RC569.5.A28 R44 2000
    616.85'8369--dc21
                            00-064454

# TABLE OF CONTENTS

# FOREWORD

Who is not a witness of ruined places?
ELLEN HINSEY, *Cities of Memory*


I want to lose myself
on the black
and silky currents,

yawning,
gathering
the tall lilies
of sleep.
MARY OLIVER, *White Night*


In this book of dreams and paintings, we, its readers, are invited to become "witness(es) of ruined places." But not only this; we are shown how to gather "the tall lilies of sleep." There is little we know about the relationship between dreaming and coming to terms with trauma, despite abundant evidence that people who have suffered trauma have repetitive and sometimes terrifying dreams. Until relatively recently, dream theory has not been closely linked with the study of trauma. Here, in *The Dreaming Way*, Patricia and Susan allow us to accompany them on a two-year journey of understanding the world of dreams in relation to trauma, an unprecedented record and commentary.

Susan's dreams themselves are riveting in their condensed metaphoric language, a language which brings both past and future into the unfolding present.

The process of dreaming reveals the ways that speaking about terrible events has been forbidden. What was unsaid and unsayable for Susan as a child (for horror is wordless and disbelief omnipresent in her betrayal), also became unspeakable. For Susan to speak as an adult woman is for her to know, to bear witness, against a legacy of forbidden speech. It is hard to overestimate her courage in attempting to understand her dreams as a process of remembering.

Susan's dreams unfold in cyclic rhythms, preparing her to bear their messages, shoring up her strength after another layer of trauma has been revealed, a testament to the dreams' power to enable her to know and to voice — in words and in paintings — what has been forbidden knowledge. It is no accident that this knowledge unfolds in the presence of a gifted listener; Patricia brings an artist's eye, as well as a broadening analysis, into relation with Susan's dreams and creative amplification. Together, they are respectful, curious, patient.

This book is particularly important at a time when there is great confusion and controversy about the nature of traumatic memories. Patricia and Susan avoid the simplicities of the current debate, through which the general public can be made to assume that memories are either completely "accurate" and "verifiable" or are "false." By documenting a careful process of recording, listening to, and responding to dreams over a long period of time, Patricia and Susan show us an entire landscape of complexly constructed associations between dreaming and memory. And, what is more, they bring us a message of hope: the heartbreaking stamina and vulnerability of trauma can be known and transformed in dreams.

Annie G. Rogers, Ph.D.

# ACKNOWLEDGEMENTS

This book has been blessed with a wholehearted spirit of collaboration from the beginning. Over the years people have lent their energy in a multitude of ways, and there are many deep bows of gratitude to be made.

To those whose generosity put a big wind in our sails we wish to thank in particular: Jan Carter, Nancy Coyne, Lisa Foley, Whitney Houghton, Mary Leibman, Ed Stern, Medora Woods, as well as our many other friends who contributed to this effort. Without their substantial help, enthusiasm, and support this project would never have been launched. The quality of friendship extended towards us and this book gave us the courage and wherewithal to proceed.

Our thanks go out to The Women's Studio Workshop in Rosendale, New York for providing us with early technical assistance and the umbrella of their non-profit organization under which the production of this book has rested. Thanks especially to Ann Kalmbach at the Women's Studio Workshop for laying out the bones of the book in its early stages. We would also like to acknowledge Jane LeCompte who provided us with her sharp editorial eye, helping us to clarify and refine our text.

A special bow of gratitude to Murray Stein of Chiron Publications for his support of this project over many years. His patient encouragement, astute recommendations, and steady hand while shepherding us through the maze of publishing requirements made the transition from manuscript to book smooth, if not effortless. Thanks also to Marisa Ten Eick who assisted with all the many details.

We would like to thank our talented and sensitive book designer Susan Kress Hamilton at Phineas for the creation and production of this book. Her enthusiasm for this project and her expertise and comradeship eased the labor of production.

We are deeply grateful to Annie G. Rogers for her interest and willingness to participate so fully in this project and for her insightful suggestion that we have the conversation, "In Retrospect," which appears at the end of the book. Her gentle wisdom helped us to bring this book home.

Finally, we have our individual acknowledgments. Patricia wishes to thank Susan for her incredible courage and integrity, for her capacity to journey deep and her ability to express what is found there. The teachings from our partnership continue to illuminate and permeate all other work. She also wishes to thank Mary Leibman for her great generosity of spirit, love, encouragement, and enduring friendship. And a heartfelt thank you goes to her partner, James Harrod, for the precious gift of his ever present love and support, his technical assistance, and for the long conversations in which he shared his deep wisdom about the dream world.

Susan would like to express her deep appreciation to Patricia for successfully and safely taking her through the dreaming recovery process. She would also like to thank her close friends who stood by her through difficult times. Susan is grateful for the love and support of her family who always believed in her as an artist, and most of all she wishes to thank her dearest husband to whom she whispered her dreams in the night.

We are both grateful for all we have been given throughout this long and arduous, wonderful and terrible process. We are especially grateful to each other and for the profound wisdom of the dreaming way.

It is a precious event when two people begin a therapeutic process together that gradually evokes a fully palpable third presence. This is how it felt to Susan and me as we began our work together. When we met, I had just opened my psychotherapy practice for women in Maine. I had spent the previous twenty years in California working as an artist, getting degrees in art and depth psychology, leading quest trips for women in the wilderness, and teaching arts and consciousness in a liberal arts program. Although I had immersed myself in the study of C.G. Jung's writings and those of others who worked with dreams, I was not aligned with any particular school or technique. I was, however, particularly interested in the power of images and image-making for healing.

Susan entered our collaboration as a working artist and a prolific dreamer, so it became clear from the start that our work would involve dreams. Since she was a visual artist, exploring the images and metaphorical nature of dreams was a natural domain for her. Her first response to her dreams was to draw them.

Anyone who works with dreams knows that the act of remembering a dream — carefully bringing it back alive and whole through the many layers of consciousness — is another art. Susan began recording her dreams by first writing them down, then drawing them in a big sketchbook. Over time she made hundreds of drawings, some of which she later translated into paintings. Susan's ability to make images of dreams joined with my training and sensibilities as a visual artist, as well as my great interest in dreams and the power of images for healing.

Each week, Susan would bring her dreams and sketchbook to my office, and we would sit on the floor and begin to open ourselves, attending as mindfully and deeply as possible to the images presented as well as to the emotions and bodily sensations evoked by the dream story. Entering into a dreamwork process together meant letting the images appear, holding the dreams and their images gently, openhandedly, reverently, in a state of trust until they revealed their messages. It was a slow, evolving work — passing the dream images back and forth, handling them like ancient treasures, listening attentively, feeling for their meaning, waiting for their hieroglyphic messages to be decoded and revealed to us. Immediately, from the very first dream that Susan brought, we began to feel the subterranean pull of the long journey ahead.

*Memory*

The dreams and images in this narrative carry deep and moving teachings about personal memory retrieval and childhood abuse recovery. They also reveal deep realms of the dream world that are concerned with healing and transformation. Susan's dreams soon presented us with some very impressive teachings about the processes of memory.

If we think about it at all, we realize that memory — the ability to recall, consciously or unconsciously, what one has learned or experienced — ensures our survival. Our instinctual knowledge, our personal identities, our kinship relations all ride on the dependability of our memory. Memory unites past and present. Memory knits together, through association, what has happened in time, so we may have a coherent and continuous sense of self. Memory provides the glue through which our life stories hang together; it gives us the integrity of our own biographies. So important was memory for the Greeks that they named Mnemosyne (Memory) Mother of the Muses. Without her, there was no art, no music, no song, no poetry, history, or dance. Human beings have always sought to understand the workings of memory, this most mysterious of our attributes.

Many of us retain the simplistic, nineteenth century notion that memory is a great record or storehouse of past information and events. This idea has its contemporary versions, too: all one has to do to remember something is go into the computer brain and bring up the lost or forgotten item from its storage file. Yet we have all had experiences of the elusive quality of memory, as well as the Rashomon type of recall where everyone has a different perspective or "memory" about an event that has happened in the past. It is this slippery aspect of memory that gives us pause and leads many to question whether we can really trust our memories as fact, as truth, as reality.

### Memory and Trauma

Anyone familiar with how the psyche works knows there are innumerable mechanisms to keep certain memories away, thereby protecting ourselves from conscious recall of past pain and terror. Although as adults we may have sequestered horrible events from our childhood, their impact is often registered on the map of our everyday lives, giving them a particular emotional tone, texture, and shape. Certain important feelings, even entire events, can be shut out from conscious memory only to exert their secret influence on our attitudes and behavior throughout our lives. Sometimes these banished memories can erupt from the depths like strange new land masses arising out of the ocean, changing our personal cartography forever. The experience of childhood trauma presents us, both survivor and witness, with that kind of experience, along with a set of difficult and unique problems, particularly around the issues of truth and memory.

One of the most critical issues for an adult survivor confronting childhood abuse is the need to fully know the truth of the trauma. Because of the psyche's protective ability to detach painful material from conscious awareness, knowledge of trauma is not always easily come by, not always a matter of simple recall. Soon after we began to work on her dreams, Susan and I were shown, in no uncertain terms, how painful, "forgotten" memories can be heaved up into consciousness through the agency of the dream world.

One of our deepest learnings from the work on this series of dreams was about the dynamic and ongoing processes of memory. We found that memory is anything but static; it is an open, complex, and integrative system. The activity of remembering can call upon and use any and all of our resources. This kind of remembering pushes across the edge of the consciously known, spans the void, and enters the "forgotten" as if it were on a crucial retrieval mission. Memory, we found, was not even time specific. It was interested not only in recalling the past, but also had things to say about the potential of the future. Rather than reducing memory to what can be proved, these dreams drew on realms that expanded our sense of what it means to remember.

Certainly we still have much to learn about the processes of memory, especially traumatic recall, which appears to be a special case. Therefore, this work does not attempt to establish dreams as a foolproof method of locating personal trauma history. It does demonstrate how, by faithfully following the dreaming process, we were shown the way toward recovery of past trauma memory, and much more. By carefully tracking the dreams for two years, we were given images from the deep realms of the dream world where lost powers are found and re-integrated, where potential future directions are indicated, and ultimately, where healing takes place.

## The Realms of the Dream World

Early on in our work, we began to notice that the dreams seemed to come from different, co-existing realms of the dreaming world. And each realm appeared to have its particular concerns and responses, its own identifiable imagery and characters, and its own specific comments to make on the process.

The various realms that were revealed to us over time included the following: the memory of actual childhood abuse events and the psyche's response to and instructions about the trauma; the emergence of an archetypal character named RED; dreams of tribal women and female initiations; and shamanic dreams with their ascents and descents, soul retrievals and animal allies and helpers. Each dream arrived from the deep reservoir of its particular realm, carefully orchestrated and precisely timed, carrying with it the exact revelation, instruction, teaching, ritual, wisdom, and healing way that was needed at the time.

## Childhood Sexual Abuse Memory

One of the first realms that appeared held the story of Susan's childhood sexual abuse, the actual traumatic events that occurred in Susan's childhood, memories of which had been shut away from her conscious recall. These dreams were accompanied by all the physical sensations, emotions, and body memories associated with remembering forgotten trauma. These dreams from the realm of personal history memory appeared throughout the work, alerting us to the actual experiences of her abuse. They were usually spaced between powerful dreams from the other realms. These other, bolstering dreams were imbued with mystery and spiritual energy, often in direct counterpoint to the trauma dreams.

## RED: The Appearance of an Archetypal Character

As the trauma dreams kept unfolding, they presented us not only with the abuse events, but also with an archetypal female dream character Susan calls RED. The emergence of RED helped us track the evolving story of abuse as well as the healing transformations that were taking place.

RED appears in many guises throughout the dream series. She was first made known to us as a "missing person." Later she appeared as a beautiful woman with "dissociated" eyes. She continued on through many shape-shifting changes. In the beginning she revealed to us the effects of the childhood trauma. She was an embodiment of wounded female sexuality — split off, false, and damaged. After a time, she arrived as a RED warrior child, full of rage toward her abuser, taking justice into her own hands, getting revenge. At one point she appeared as Scarlett O'Hara. Then her presence was made known simply by the deep sensual quality of the color RED. As she became more integrated and connected, she appeared as a full, vibrant, sexual woman, and the color RED was complemented by other significant colors, like black and white.

The dream realms concerned with the childhood trauma and the archetypal dream figure, RED, took us through all the stages of abuse recovery. We became students of this dream realm as it showed us precisely where we needed to place our attention. The need for the truth to be known, to be spoken and believed, the need for witnesses, the desire for revenge on the abuser, the sadness and grief over the loss of childhood innocence, the regaining of female power — all of these came through at this dreaming level, bringing us the necessary awareness, giving us the keys, the way into the story and through it to the threshold of recovery.

One very important dream in the middle of the process helped us see that we were on the right track. In this dream Susan was literally "finding all the pieces" of her childhood trauma story, digging them out of the ground and showing them to her family. From this dream, we were able to consider actually breaking silence with her family in the waking world.

### Tribal Initiation

The third dream realm that made itself known was a place of female initiation signaled by the appearance of tribal women. These dreams started at the very beginning of our work together and led us to believe that the dream world holds "tribal memory." We are using "tribal memory" here to indicate those dreams that appeared to draw on female initiatory and ritual actions and healings.

From the paintings in the Paleolithic caves of Europe and Africa, we know that artistic renderings were important parts of our early ancestors' lives. Along with these visual representations, tribal cultures developed oral traditions and rituals through which memory passes down the generations, creating a body of knowledge and wisdom on which the culture can draw. One of the great losses in our present culture is collective ceremony and story for the purposes of healing. The forms available to us today in organized religion, although developed over centuries, often seem to lack the ability to touch the depths of the soul, particularly where trauma is concerned. Even more lacking in today's world are rituals that attend to the traumatic events in women's lives. However, our dreams are still a repository for these medicine ways, compensating for the dearth of ritual practices in our culture. If we attend carefully, dreams can offer healing, honoring, and celebration of our place in the community of women.

From this dream realm of "tribal memory," we learned that the impulse toward group ritual and initiation is as old as human consciousness. This realm brings with it the transformational power inherent in ritual actions. To undergo a healing rite in a dream is as impressive and real as anything could be. Susan's dreams of tribal women show that the power to draw on healing traditions and practices, even if lacking in our culture, is still available to us through the "tribal memory" of the dream world. These dreams were usually concerned with revitalizing female powers. They were intimate in nature, nurturing and energizing.

### Shamanic Healing

The fourth dream realm that presented itself was the shamanic level of healing. It is closely related to the realm of "tribal memory," yet it is different in content and feeling.

There has been a great resurgence of interest in and study of shamanism in the last twenty years. In one of the most important texts on shamanism, historian of religion Mircea Eliade notes that the shaman is indispensable in any ceremony that concerns the experiences of the human soul. Eliade says that "the shaman performs the function of doctor and healer; he announces the diagnosis, goes in search of the patient's fugitive soul, captures it, and makes it return to animate the body that it has left." Since the soul, Eliade says, is "a precarious psychic unit, inclined to forsake the body" it becomes "an easy prey for demons and sorcerers."

Anyone who works with dreams, their own and those of others, will recognize that there are some dreams that can bear the designation shamanic. The shamanic traditions have always been about deep, ecological restoration and healing, and so it is no surprise that elements and patterns from the shamanic level of human experience enter our dreams when there is injury. What is surprising, of course, is their unbidden appearance in the dreams of people who live in a culture so far removed from that source of knowledge.

A number of dreams in this series exhibited traditional shamanic methods of healing. Shamanic practices around the world share technologies for establishing contact with the sacred. In this series of dreams, descents to the underworld and ascents to the upper world were undertaken; soul retrievals took place; connections were made with powers from the natural world; dream "spirit helpers" gave assistance; and medicine animals lent their tremendous powers and energy. We feel that these dreams were drawn from earth-based healing traditions. They came from the shamanic wisdom of the dream world.

It is important to note here that although I had read a great deal about various types of shamanism, neither of us were engaged in any shamanic practices. It seems clear from this series of dreams that the shamanic realm of healing is available and operative even for those without shamanic training. The dream world has a shamanic memory that the psyche can draw on. It was up to us, as students of the dream, to make the connections between the shamanic realm and contemporary life.

## The Way of the Dream

Susan's dreams were an impending invitation to both of us to enter the mysterious depths of the dreaming world. The way of the dream not only revealed knowledge of Susan's personal psyche, but also touched the outer reaches of human and other-than-human consciousness, the great sensorium of our collective experience. The dream world manifested itself to us as a co-extensive, intricately constructed, engaged and animated, multi-dimensional reality. It resonated and responded to our willingness to open to its wisdom.

The dreams were both sequential and cyclic. They moved along in an unfolding way, yet had a definite cyclical rhythm. Over the course of time, we found there to be a distinct pattern to the dreams' content. The very difficult and emotionally wrenching dreams that were concerned with recalling missing pieces of Susan's childhood abuse story were frequently introduced by or followed by strengthening dreams, dreams coming from a place infused with energy, mystery, and power. Where the rejected, unadmitted, unrecognized realities awaited us, there, too, the powers of the spirit offered us stamina and courage to proceed. The whole period of dreaming, drawing, painting, and dreamwork yielded a vast, yet coherent, view of the dream world at work.

In the dreams from this two-year period in Susan's life, she moved through unimagined landscapes; the night sky opened, and trees lit up with moving stars. She entered caves from ancient times and learned how she must live; she was shown vivid images of her own personal suffering; she was taken on night sea journeys; she found spirit guides. She met grand and mysterious lovers and took revenge on those who had hurt her; she reunited with loved ones and raised the dead. She witnessed and participated in female tribal initiation rituals.

Animals came to her aid, bringing their deep instinctual knowledge and wisdom to bear on her situation. A wild windhorse arrived to be her companion; a great, protective bear lumbered through; blue thunderbirds streaked the sky, and small birds landed on her palms; lizards climbed on her shoulder; and crocodiles lay in wait. In these dreams the natural world responded. The earth quaked; the dark funnel of a tornado was glimpsed; a flood occurred.

The dreams were evocative and sensate, full of body and feeling. Susan underwent; she was afflicted; she endured; she opened. As the dreams pulled on all possible and impossible imagery, so, too, our responses to them drew on all levels of our being — biological, psychological and spiritual.

Working intensely with the dreams over this two-year period, we became aware of a guiding intelligence at work. This was what we call the third presence. It gave us an identifiable pace, where themes from the different realms appeared and disappeared, only to reappear in another form. We got the sense of motion, intention, unfoldment. The dreamer's tasks were revealed, and we felt the dreams working to help us accomplish them. We were shown the richness of imagery drawn from the various realms of the dreaming world; the dream's impeccable sense of story and plot; a variety of characters both demonic and angelic, ordinary and archetypal. Helpful allies arrived precisely when they were most needed. And most especially, we were shown the dream world's insistent, self-correcting, and healing direction. This work at times scared us, bewildered us, moved us, and profoundly impressed and humbled us both.

## The Way of the Artist

Susan recorded many, many dreams throughout the two years we worked together. She has twelve large, black drawing books filled with her dream drawings. She made her paintings from the original sketches, usually after we worked through the dream's content. Often a painting was made months later. Susan discovered that the process of making paintings can uncover whole other layers of meaning related to the dream images. When she brought the paintings into my office, we would go back over the dream and the original sketches and find that the painting held additional information and insight and deeply enriched our understanding. Susan explains this process more fully in the Conclusion.

For this book, we selected the drawings and paintings that we felt were most pertinent to the issues of childhood sexual trauma and that gave a cohesive and coherent story of her recovery process. Dreams in general, like any deep story or myth, offer us endless possible interpretations and meanings. We know there may be other, different, equally valid renderings of the following dreams. We are presenting what we found in our work together, given our mutual states of emotional, psychological, intellectual, and spiritual development.

## The Dreams of a Woman

It seems significant to note that the dreams recorded here are the dreams of a woman, and that the dreamwork took place within the container made by us as two women working together. Recent research from dream labs shows that women's dreams differ from men's, a difference arising in part from physiological make-up and in part from differing experiences and responses to our culture and collective history. Perhaps these factors cannot be completely assigned to gender, because as these dreams show, there is also a large dose of mystery. But from our experience with these dreams, it does seem important that we learn to attend differently to the dreams of women and men in order to hear and see more fully what the dream world has to offer from each perspective. The dream realms from which these dreams are drawn do seem to point and attend, in very specific and notable ways, to what can only be called a female transformation process.

## Dreamwork and Art as Rituals for Healing

For Susan, this process became one of honoring dreams as truth. Truth, like memory, is not simple. It is complex and integrative. The dreams, drawings, and paintings gave us truth — not truth as proof, but truth as emergent, changing, instructive and crucial knowing. They gave us truth as embodied and experiential, precise and congruent understanding.

Through the doorway of dreams, with the support of our alliance, we entered the realms of the unconscious. There, the memory of Susan's childhood sexual abuse became known to her. This process was often terrifying and frequently felt beyond our conscious control. By drawing and painting her dreams, Susan grounded her reality. By fully engaging with her dreams, she was challenged to accept great pain, and eventually, the reality of her childhood trauma story. Despite the demands made on her by the dreams, Susan responded with artistic expression, and she was rewarded for her efforts. The characters and creatures who appeared from the various dream realms and evolved in her paintings gave her the opportunity to see herself not only as a victim and survivor, but also as a rich, full, multi-aspected woman.

It goes without saying that the work we did for two years in the consulting room was much more detailed and specific to Susan's personal life and to our working relationship. We did not think it necessary for our purposes in this book to present more particular identifying material. We wish to honor the sanctity of the personal space we made together, the container into which the dreams so generously and abundantly flowed. Our therapeutic working relationship always involved the third presence of the images — the dream world, the sketches, and the paintings — and this is where our attention was primarily focused.

After two years of intensive exploration, the dreams began to change in content, direction, and intensity. They took up other themes. We began to feel that the major piece of work around her childhood abuse that the dreams had initiated was moving toward completion. Because the dreams had given us such a rich, vivid, and deeply moving experience of healing, we felt moved to share this process. This prospect opened another piece of work as our relationship widened to include the possibility of presenting this work to various audiences, and eventually, over the course of more than ten years, to produce this book.

We have presented the dreams in the sequence in which they occurred. Although some of the paintings were made later, sometimes much later, the dreams are dated and put in the order in which they were dreamed and worked. Where it is pertinent, we note in our commentary when a painting was made.

*19*

## Another View

Much has been written about childhood sexual abuse in the last two decades. We have learned a great deal about the frequency of occurrence and its impact on the survivor. The therapeutic community and the culture at large are in an enormous upheaval over the unspeakable reality that so many children have been and are being so misused and mistreated. Despite the high levels of awareness and the consciousness-raising over the last twenty years, we are still involved in the project of understanding not only how to stop the abuse of children, but also how to help alleviate the suffering of those who have been traumatized. Despite great efforts on the part of many people, there is still more to learn, new ways to listen and respond to trauma and its terrible teachings.

The study of sexual abuse trauma comes to us from two sources: the therapeutic community, which focuses on the pathology, the mental disorders and behavioral disturbances that are the signature of early childhood abuse; and the numerous survivor narratives and stories, through which we come to know the world of childhood trauma and its effects on the victim. These two separate but necessarily related sources have their own agendas, language, and ethos, yet each fills out the other's authority. Together, they make up the whole of literature on abuse trauma.

This book brings another view. Here survivor and witness are at work together. The medium through which we communicate is dreams, amplified by drawings and paintings of dreams and their associations. In this collaboration, survivor and witness are joined in a process of revelation and recovery in which both the personal and transpersonal levels of healing and teaching are made manifest. The dreamwork and art presented here represent our exploration along the path of the dreaming way. This book is intended to be both an honoring of what we have discovered and a contribution to the wider community of dreamers and dreamworkers.

Those of you who have worked or are working on your own personal trauma history, and those of you who make a life's work of partnering with people in the practice of psychotherapy, can draw hope and inspiration from this work. When we began it, we had no way of knowing what would unfold. We adopted an attitude of respectful partnership with the dreams. They became our teacher and we their students. Even in working with this material over ten years later, we find that there is more to learn. We invite you to enter this dreamtime for your own instruction, drawing on the dream world's wisdom for your own enrichment and healing.

# THE DREAMING WAY

*I have missed my plane. A man offers to drive me, because he doesn't think I can make it on my own. I become angry and turn him down. I get on a train with six women. We become poor black women. We don't have tickets and are thrown off the train. We go to prison where we are beaten and abused. We must put on men's clothing to blend in and survive. Through the railyard, we find our way out. Once we are on the train, our clothes become African tribal women's clothes. We are still black, and we are proud of our heritage.*

## "Queen of the Night"
### FEBRUARY 16, 1987

SUSAN

*In this dream I refuse to be escorted and insist on making my own way. I go with the women on the train. We are poor and have no tickets. It is a spiral down from there. In the prison the male inmates beat us because we are women. The men's clothing is our camouflage. There is pain and adaptation. We escape through the railyard dressed as men. When our ordeal is over, we transform into our tribal selves, one of whom is the Queen of the Night. She is all seeing and all knowing. Feeling her presence means safety and security. I feel I am being shown an initiation of survival and must honor it and reflect upon it.*

This is the first dream that Susan and I worked on together. C.G. Jung often noted that the first dream a person brought into the therapeutic work was significant, and usually diagnostic. This dream gives us an immediate sense that there will be something to endure, a difficult passage, an initiation. It also lets us know that the ordeal will be survived, the lost power restored.

In the opening part of the dream, there are various means of travel. But the plane is missed, and the offer of a ride is not taken. There is anger about the man's insinuation that the dreamer lacks the ability to make it, and she gets on the train with other women.

This dream, where the black women first make their appearance, tracks the loss of tribal female power. The dream sequence tells about a time of diminishment, impoverishment, and subjugation. In the beginning the power of the women is already depleted. They are just a small group of poor black women stripped of any empowering, enabling, or ennobling identifiers. Their poverty, their lack of resources, makes them susceptible to mistreatment. They are unable to make the journey in any privileged way; they have no tickets, and with no negotiable way to pass, they are thrown off the train that would take them home.

Like the Jews in Exodus, or African-Americans in our culture, they undergo an ordeal of exile, a time of tribulation. Their original identities are stripped from them; they are denied their freedom and become slaves in another's land. They find a strategy for survival commonly used by oppressed peoples everywhere; they put on their oppressors' clothing. In other words, they begin to make an identification with their persecutors, and this move offers them the protection of camouflage so they can find their way out of their situation. Once they get back on the train with other women suddenly they are liberated — dressed again in their tribal clothes, their collective female power and heritage reclaimed, their pride restored. These black women appear from the dream world not only as representatives of oppression, they carry empowering energy as well.

Something emerges from this survival initiation — the "Queen of the Night," with her tribal clothes, her power made visible, her vision and knowledge evident, her strength apparent. Susan honors her appearance in the dream by painting her in full regalia. The "Queen of the Night" stands as the guardian, the seer, the one who knows. We have the sense that she will be the one to watch over the process and any ordeals to come.

*The* horses have arrived from Portugal. They are in the stalls, wild and beautiful. We are afraid to let them out — they are supercharged.

# "Horse Sense"

FEBRUARY 22, 1987

## SUSAN

*My horse energy is boxed up in the stalls. The horses are so powerful and wild that I am afraid to let them out. The red horse feels like the power of fire and passion, the black horse like the power of night and the unconscious.*

## PATRICIA

These horses give us feelings of impressive physical power. Their appearance signals a great import of energy. They also seem to be showing us a split in instinctual lifeforce. There are two of them, one black, one red; they are untamed and unrelated at this point, having just arrived. They are so powerful that the only thing that keeps them together is the stalls. We wonder if the dream may be playing with the word "stall" as there is quite a bit of ambivalence about this influx of power and a lot of questions about why these horses appear now and how their energy can be made accessible.

I am made curious by the arrival of these magnificent horses and wonder what kind of powers they hold. Are they work horses? Race horses? Will Susan be able to use this energy? How do we go about getting into relationship with them?

From my reading of Mircea Eliade and his work on shamanism, I learn that when humankind domesticated the horse, we were no longer earthbound; we could bond with the fleet, four-footed creatures and fly like the wind. Because of their power and swiftness, horses are thought to be the premier shamanic animal, allowing the shaman to ride the wind of the upper world. Eliade notes that the dominant mythology of the horse is funerary. The horse carries the deceased into the beyond; it produces the "breakthrough in plane," making the passage from this world to other worlds. This leads me to see that these horses have the potential to connect with the dead places, the place of lost souls. They are raring to go. Questions remain, however. Can we make connection and establish communication with this powerful energy source? Can Susan learn to harness the horse energy and make it usable for her journey? For now all we know is that the energy is there, ready to burst out.

*My friend and I go to a drawing group session. She brings her son. He drinks a can of Orange Crush and dies. I must go and comfort her. The dream feeling is wrenchingly sad.*

## "The Black Hole"
### APRIL 17, 1987

SUSAN

*I recognize the woman in this dream drawing from waking life. She is my best friend and is also an artist. Recently she revealed to me that she is in the process of recovering childhood incest memories. As she talked to me, my chest became tight and my breath felt shallow and constricted.*

*When Patricia and I work with this disturbing dream drawing in a session, the characters begin to shift in relationship to me. First, I think the dream is about my friend. Then, I realize that the dream is about me. It is MY dream. I feel a deep shudder of recognition and identification with the artist/incest survivor. In the dream the child is given Orange Crush for pain, a drink once given to me by a doctor in waking life. I recognize myself as the child who drinks and dies in the dream, and then I begin to see the artist/survivor as my own mother. Who, then, is the man asleep on the couch? If I am the child, I sense he is the grandfather; if I am the mother, he becomes my father. Following this there is only blackness and the dawning realization that I had been sexually abused by someone in my family. I experience confusion and intense fear and anxiety with this dream. I know it is the beginning of something very terrifying.*

*The feeling of blackness is a deep sucking down energy that pulls me to an*

26

*unknown place. The black hole feels so deep, I fear I will not re-emerge. When fear breaks the plunge, I surface and breathe once again.*

*I have no control over this feeling. The dizziness follows me on the street, while driving the car, in restaurants. My legs shake, and I feel short of breath. It is only in the presence of Patricia that I feel safe enough to fall into that black space. I want her to touch my hand to keep me connected to the present, so I know I will be coming back. I feel that the falling is dying, disappearing, and I am afraid. But I also know that knowledge and memory are only recovered at the bottom of the black space.*

## PATRICIA

The appearance of this dream — the emotions, the physical sensations, and the drawing — begin the process of remembering. In the dream, the dreamer is struck with deep emotional and physical feelings, a combination of fear and knowing. Her dizziness, shortness of breath, and shaking legs I recognize as the sensate workings of deep memory. When Susan and I work on this dream drawing together, we both feel dizzy, as if we were being pulled down by some tremendous force. For Susan it is the vertiginous pull of the "black hole" of trauma; for me, it is an empathic bodily response alerting me to the fact that we are being drawn into the gap, the void, the place of lost memory. We experienced this joint vertigo whenever we were drawn deeply into the place of repressed trauma. It was critically important that we "stay in touch" with each other especially at these times. Sometimes it was actual physical touching — reaching out to touch each other's hand; other times we verbally affirmed what we were experiencing, and reassured ourselves by taking a breath before we continued.

In Susan's drawing we are shown varying degrees of awareness: on the one hand, there is the unconscious man on the couch; then there is the awake mother on her knees behind the child. She is holding something. Susan says the mother is holding out one of Susan's drawings. What does the mother know? The child is given something to narcotize, to quiet her pain. Does the mother give the child the drink? The cup the child is drinking from is placed right over the crotch of the sleeping man. Does the mother pass on her way of forgetting to the child? The dream says, "the child 'dies' from it." In other words, the child-awareness is being lost, numbed out, repressed.

The furniture in this drawing takes on importance. We notice that whenever there is an issue to be looked at, Susan includes a table in her drawing. With the appearance of the table, we learn to become alert to the fact that something needs to be "put on the table." The lamp in the drawing has light emanating from it, urging us to cast the light of our awareness on this sad scene.

From this dream we are left with the definite feeling that something terrible has happened. But there are many questions. Is the dream only about her mother, or is Susan implicated, too? The emotions and physical sensations continue after the dream, dogging Susan in her waking life. We are put on alert.

*27*

*D*riving in my convertible, I stop by a gateway of some stone ruins in the desert. There is a wooden box full of lizards, "leapin' lizards." They were almost out of their box. They were funny and scary.

# "Leapin' Lizards!"
### APRIL 28,1987

## SUSAN

*In my dreams lizards are generally small and green. Here, they are humorous little ones, bumping and struggling to free themselves from the box. The caged energy of the lizards feels similar to the wild horses caught in the stalls. Clearly, something needs to be released.*

## PATRICIA

The physical energy of the lizards leaves us with a wiggly, anticipatory feeling. Susan feels these creatures are her intuitions, once boxed up, now ready to burst out.

Turning to the images from the dream, we focus on the gateway that leads into the stone ruins. This image seems to indicate an entryway into the remaining foundations of an old structure, something from the past. The box of lizards is at the gateway. Although they are cold-blooded saurians connected with the oldest part of our brain — the reptilian brain — these lizards are not particularly menacing. They just want "out." I wonder whether their appearance, after the previous dream, is announcing the opening up of some very archaic material. Susan's title for this dream is "Leapin' Lizards!," an exclamation of surprise made by Little Orphan Annie, communicating her mixed feelings of funny and scared.

*A*n invasion force is coming. There are animals in cages under the cave edge. We are going to connect the pigs together in a barricade. Below is an army of horsemen lined up four across. I know we have elephants. I go down the mesa with swords. I cut off legs and arms; then I am shocked at my behavior and stop.

# *"The Grand Matriarch"*

## APRIL 30, 1987

### SUSAN

*This dream tells me I am in big trouble, and I must call upon my allies for assistance. Connecting the pigs in a barricade seems comical to me. My elephants are huge and black; they fortify my position. In my drawing book I have written: "Too much Violence," commenting on my actions in the dream. Cutting off arms and legs is a way to incapacitate the soldiers without killing them, but the violence stops because I am shocked and horrified by what I have done. The action does seem manic — a frantic attempt to take over the invasion force and prevent it from happening. I take this dream as a metaphor of a bloody battle to come, in which there will be deaths and injury.*

### PATRICIA

This dream, two days after the last one where the lizards are breaking out of their box, warns us and deepens our awareness that we are in for an invasion, an assault from some part of the dreaming world. We do not yet know who the intruding "enemy" is, but there is a great sense of preparation. The psyche is marshalling tremendous forces, enormous energies are being gathered to withstand the onslaught.

The images of dismemberment — the chopping off of arms and legs — seem, as Susan says, a manic attempt to stave off the inevitable. The pig barricade is a first line of defense. It is clear that the pigs are not a ferocious means of protection; they are strictly sacrificial animals, an offering to the gods of war. Elephants, on the other hand, have historically been used as powerful allies in warfare. I tell Susan that for the Hindus, the elephant-headed god Ganesha is the ultimate victor over obstacles. Susan feels these elephants are the great matriarchs, the maternal protectors. They have come to lend her their strength so she can draw on their power for the battle to come. After we have worked on the dream, she honors them by making a painting of one of them.

$T$here is a body covered with leaves in the sandbox. Encapsulated bees float over her and sting her. She raises up.

# "Rebirth"

MAY 1, 1987

## S U S A N

*This is my wonderful mulch pile from which life returns. From a pile of refuse, the mulch pile is able to regenerate itself into valuable black gold, a nutrient rich growing medium. The dream feels like a resurrection because it follows the preceding dream of death and destruction. In the painting, I made the sandbox red to signify life. This feels like a dream of hope.*

## P A T R I C I A

The dream image announces a coming back to life, a re-emergence of a life force energy that once was buried. It was a signal to us that the battle to the death in the preceding dream was somehow going to be won and that the reward would be this emerging female energy. The quick sharp pain of the bees' stings stimulates the renewal of life, giving the same kind of pain we feel when some part of our body "falls asleep" and starts to come back to life. This dream puts me in mind of Sylvia Plath's poem "Lady Lazarus," about a woman's power to regenerate herself, to raise herself from the dead.

*I* *am in an apartment with my mother and grandmother. A cracked vase of flowers is sent to me. Mom and Grandma admire the flowers but do not notice that the vessel is fractured.*

# "Fractured Vessel"

MAY 1, 1987

## SUSAN

*Hugh Hefner once sent these flowers to a woman I know. The cracked vase feels like an image of a wounded female sexual body. My mother and grandmother are unable to see the brokenness and the pain. The beauty of the flowers is masking the damage to the vessel. The cracked vase appears to me as a body and spirit metaphor.*

## PATRICIA

This dream presents us with a strong image of the fracturing effects of trauma and how easily they can be overlooked within the family. The vase as body-vessel for the spirit is cracked right down the middle; it cannot adequately hold life-sustaining water. Although their beauty is admirable, the flowers are not going to last; they, too, are cut off.

In the painting Susan has put the vase on a pedestal. One way a woman can lose track of herself is by being put on a pedestal. Although it may seem a kind of honoring and respect it is really an idealizing that denies real pain and suffering. As in the "Black Hole" dream, there is reference to Susan's female lineage — grandmother, mother, daughter. In the dream, the inability of these older women to see their own suffering creates their denial of Susan's broken vase and causes a further sense of wounding to the daughter. This image shows the poignant state of a woman who has had any kind of sexual wounding: she may be able to mask her pain, and others may deny it, but the soul container has registered the damage.

*I'm given an ice-blue car. Inside there are long red gloves, a red dress, and red shoes.*

# "Invitation to Red"

MAY 17, 1987

## SUSAN

*I was really excited by this dream and wanted to know, Who wears the red clothes? To find out, I meditated deeply on the red items and called to the one who wears them. This was the only time I ever used the active imagination method for consciously recreating a dream state.*

*I waited for a response. She came to me: the woman who wears red. When I made her image, I could see that she was sad and isolated. I could also see that she held passion in her wild hair and red-clothed body, but her eyes were disassociated. Her message to me was to set her free — open the door to the closet and let her out. I became aware that, throughout my waking life, it was this "RED" who had frequently broken out and caused havoc in my relationships. It is clear from this encounter with her that she needs a place to be, and I want her more integrated into the whole of my being.*

## PATRICIA

Susan was made curious and excited by the mystery of this missing person. Who has left her RED clothes behind? In the painting Susan made, the dream car is ice-blue, which indicates that there is a coldness in the way the woman in the red clothes has gotten around in the world. Now, the car door is flung wide open, but the woman is missing. By leaving her clothes behind, she has given Susan a clue. This release of energy allowed Susan to invite RED to appear, first through a process of active imagination and then by letting her emerge in a painting.

Active imagination is a dreamwork technique discovered by C. G. Jung. It entails contacting images or characters from dreams by using one's imagination and recording what transpires. It is a way of "dreaming the dream onward." By using this technique, Susan was able to gain more information about RED which she then put into her painting of her. The painting process itself adds another dimension.

RED's appearance is one of the first indications that there is a split-off dream personality who embodies her wounded female sexuality. The act of bringing RED to awareness through active imagination and painting lets Susan become more familiar with her. She feels her loneliness and isolation; she notices RED's "disassociated eyes." This gives some indication that RED has been traumatized. She also sees that there is passionate wildness in her hair, but like the flowers in the cracked vase, RED is in a brittle, cut-off, weakened state. Any split-off part of ourselves, any uninte-grated aspect, leaves us feeling fragile and vulnerable, and this is the case with RED.

RED's first appearance as a fragmented persona reminds me of Lawrence Langer's description of how, in the concentration camps, people would develop what he calls an "impromptu self." This "impromptu self" is created out of moral chaos; it is severed from the nourishing roots of the integrated self by traumatic circumstances. Later, in survivor testi-monies, the "impromptu self" appears as a kind of "violated self," a source of chagrin and humiliation, a seemingly self-violated self. RED, I feel, could be called an "impromptu self" for Susan. Although at this point in our work we do not know her whole story, we do realize that she is a partial and improvised character designed to give us an introduction to the one who holds both the passion and the pain of injured female sexu-ality. We are very glad to meet her.

*A big barn door opens. There is a huge, wooden, barge-like wagon inside with draft horses to pull it. A large, silent driver backs the rig out of the barn. We get in and ride slowly, passing over the bridge. The dogs guard each side of the bridge; they are the pullers of the barge.*

# "The Guardians"
## JULY 2, 1987

## SUSAN

*The barn is deep and dark. There is no sense of fear in the dream, only a readiness and anticipation for the journey. The driver is a mystery man. The slow passing is purposeful and deliberate. My guardians are flanking the bridge and I know I am safe to proceed. The dogs will pull the barge through the dark night where the dream is taking me — somewhere very important. I completely trust that this is the way to go there.*

## PATRICIA

This dream carries a very deep and mysterious image. I recognize it as a classic night sea journey dream with the silent Charon figure, the ferryman, who transports the souls of the dead to the other world. These journeys or descents to the underworld are not strictly about taking souls to their final destination. They are undertaken especially for retrieval, to find and bring back a lost part of a sick person's soul.

Because of the mythological feel of this dream, I go back to Eliade's book and read about shamanistic descents into the underworld. There are two defining characteristics, he says, dogs and the "porter" or ferryman who carries the souls. The motif of the bridge can also be present. Dogs are often described mythologically as healing and protecting escorts into the Beyond. In Susan's dream they are both guardians of the threshold and pullers of the wagon-barge. The "porter," from the shamanic traditions or the Charon figure from Greek mythology, ferries the soul to its destination.

In Susan's dream the silence feels crucial. When an initiation into a great mystery is undertaken, silence is demanded. The underworld journey also takes us away from the realm of words. Communication happens on another plane. The bridge indicates a crossing over, a bridging of the realms. Eliade notes that in shaman tales of descent, the bridge connects two cosmic regions and signifies passing from one mode of being to another — "from uninitiate to initiate." In some versions of the crossing it is told that the "guilty" cannot cross and are precipitated into the abyss.

We feel from this dream that we are entering a very deep part of the journey. The silent purposefulness lends an aura of deep intention. Despite the potentially ominous atmosphere, Susan's sense of safety and my sense of trust enable us to align ourselves with the dream's direction and intent.

*There is a goddess on a pedestal. She has taken off her shoes and is breaking from her pose. She is waiting for her stone replacement. She is the goddess of well-being. I know her name is "Ariadne." The statue was first a woman, then a stone, and then a woman again.*

## "Ariadne"
JULY 4, 1987

S U S A N
*When I awoke from this dream, the name "Ariadne" was on my lips. I said this name over and over. I did not know who she was or why I spoke*

*her name. The goddess on the pedestal is standing in the passageway to the sea. She bends down and removes her shoes. She is ready to depart but must wait for her stone replacement. She was first a woman, then a stone, then a woman again. I see this image as one of my own transformation through this dreaming, healing process.*

## PATRICIA

This dream is one of those that reminds us that we all have a mythic memory. Although Susan was not consciously aware of the myth of Ariadne, her dreamer knew and introduced this mythic figure into her story. Being a student of myth myself, I knew that Ariadne is one of the pre-Hellenic forms of Aphrodite, the goddess of love. It is Ariadne who holds the thread as Theseus makes the rebirth journey through the labyrinth — a womb journey to the center of the soul and back. Ariadne is also the emblem of the abandoned woman. Betrayed by her lover Theseus, abandoned on the island of Naxos, Ariadne was left to suffer her "death into rebirth." In her suffering Ariadne is transformed from mortal woman to goddess. I was, of course, amazed that Susan's dreamer found this particular image to give us an accurate reading of where we were in the process.

Again, we have the image of the pedestal, now even more elaborated and personified than the one on which the fractured vase stood. Ariadne stands on the pedestal, frozen in place, her energies inaccessible and unavailable. There are many myths and stories about people being frozen, turned to stone, usually as a punishment for some transgression. Lot's wife was turned to a pillar of salt as she was leaving Sodom and Gomorrah. Her sin was curiosity, looking back. The goddess in Susan's dream seems to have gotten frozen from holding her "pose." She may be an image of the "impromptu self," a persona manufactured out of trauma. She may also be an image of frozen feeling, fixed in her position. There is some assurance that she was not always this way; she was a woman before she turned to stone. Now, she begins to come back to life, breaking her pose, waiting for her stone replacement.

The landscape of this dream is also important. Ariadne is standing at the gateway or passageway to the sea, the unconscious deeps. She cannot enter them as a stone; she would sink. So she has to wait for her stone replacement. It seems that the psyche is telling us that in order to begin the journey into the unconscious, one has to be a bit warm, human, with feeling. This dream shows us another necessary preparation for making the journey.

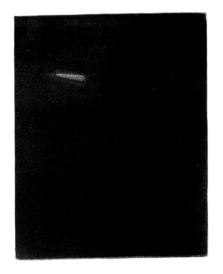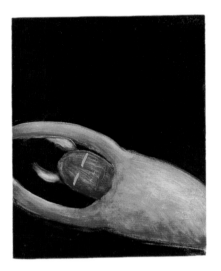

*I* *show my artwork. I have a children's book. The open page of the*
*book shows a deep purple velvet space with a rocket and a beast crossing*
*the void.*

## "Shaman and Sputnik"
### JULY 5, 1987

SUSAN
*There is a feeling of searching and wandering in this dream image. The*
*purple void is a seductive space. I suspect the children's book is connect-*
*ed to the mystery of my own childhood story.*

PATRICIA
The deep purple velvet space in this dream fascinated and mystified us
and continues to do so. It conveys the experience of such deep space
that it can hardly be articulated. Susan feels it is seductive, drawing us
into its mystery.

Susan calls this dream "Shaman and Sputnik," and that gives us a clue to its meaning. Again, I go back to Eliade. He says that one of the shaman's great tasks is to restore the "communicability" between heaven and earth, to bridge "the break between the planes." Shamans, he tells us, tend to travel in two directions: a descent to the underworld, as we noted in the prior dream; and an ascent to the heavenly realms, as in this dream. Both journeys are undertaken for the purposes of restoration, to retrieve lost souls. Eliade says the shaman can roam vast distances, penetrating the underworld and rising to the sky, because the shaman has been initiated into these "extraterrestrial regions." The danger of losing his way in these forbidden regions is still great. "But sanctified by his initiation and furnished with his guardian spirits, the shaman is the only human being able to challenge the danger and venture into a mystical geography."

It seems to us that this notion can also apply interpsychically and that certain dreams are meant to do this reconnecting work between the conscious and the unconscious worlds. In particular, when there is abuse trauma that has been repressed and "forgotten," the dream itself acts as the shaman who makes the "difficult passage" into the void, or the world of the dead, the place of forgotten memory. The dream does this in order to bring "lost" memory back to our consciousness, helping us restore communication, giving us a renewed sense of integrity and congruity.

Translated into psychological language, we could say that trauma, which causes parts of the psyche to fragment, dissociate, or split off from the physical body, creates a condition similar to what Eliade describes. Spiritually speaking, we can talk about how a part of the soul tends to leave the body when confronted with terrible treatment; it is necessary to retrieve that piece of soul so healing and re-integration can take place. The "Shaman and Sputnik" is an example of just such a retrieval mission.

In Susan's painting the shaman has a mask-like face and is equipped with horns. I remember that "sputnik" is the Russian name for the satellites sent into space to collect information. I look up the definition and find that the word "sputnik" means "companion," and has associations with a Sanskrit word meaning "way, path or course." The dream image shows that the sputnik, a companion to the process, is headed out into cosmic space, and the shaman reaches out for it, opening a channel for information to come back to us. We feel it is a modern image taken from Susan's early childhood, the time when a piece of her soul may have split off into outer space due to traumatic events. I am reminded that the shaman bridges the realms to establish communication between heaven and earth. The "Shaman and Sputnik," an apt name for the creature in this dream and its mission, are assisting us by bringing the child's soul-story back to earth.

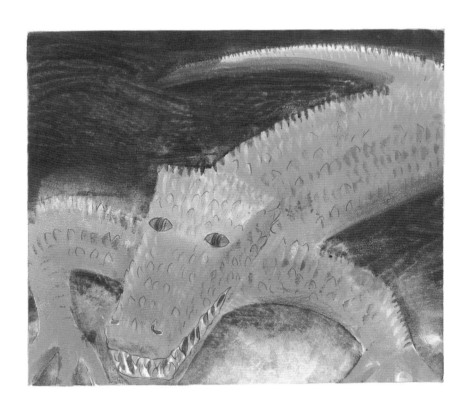

*I am riding a crocodile by the tail. I am afraid to let go; I am afraid to hold on.*

# "Crocodile Ride"

## AUGUST 18, 1987

SUSAN

*If I let go, I will be eaten; if I hold on, I will drown. I am truly stuck. In my life, at this moment, I cannot move ahead. Fear is preventing me from facing myself. Facing the truth feels like dying.*

PATRICIA

This dream describes a pivotal moment in our work, a feeling of "choice-less choice" where both possibilities feel annihilating. From the outer reaches of the deep void of cosmic space in the last dream, Susan is now plunged into the underwater deeps with its terrible dangers. She has the crocodile by the tail; she has gotten hold of something, and now she must either hold on or let go. Crocodiles, I tell her, especially in Egyptian mythology, such as "The Book of the Dead," are terrible guardians of the Bardo, the place of dead souls. Spells and incantations of riddance and banishment are necessary. Making the image helps. The colors in this painting are noteworthy: the sickening green on a background of deep red.

*T*here is samurai warfare with swords and shields. They are looking for the beautiful wife of the hero warrior. She has been with her lover and is in disgrace. They have captured her. She bends her white neck forward, wraps her head in her sleeve, and prepares for her death by the sword.

# "Surrender"

OCTOBER 2, 1987

## S U S A N

*In surrendering to the truth, I must be willing to symbolically die — to give up addictions, to give up lies, to face what is left. It is not clear where the path will lead, but it is necessary to trust that I must go there. The woman in the dream willingly submits to the blade, as I am submitting to this process as it unfolds.*

## P A T R I C I A

Here is the dream's answer to the crocodile ride dilemma. This image of surrender brought with it a feeling of deep submission, not necessarily to something harmful or punishing, but more to the sword of truth. There is little fear or struggle in this dream; instead, there is preparation and a willingness to face her fate. The graceful gesture of lifting her hair in order to bare her beautiful white neck is a signal that the dream woman will make and accept the sacrifice. By renouncing old destructive patterns and letting go of her habitual thoughts, beliefs, and attitudes, Susan submits to some deeper truth within the psyche. Severing the head with the sword of truth indicates a need to release her mind from its old constructs, its worn out ways of construing the world. It is a radical act intended to end resistance, confusion, and self-doubt in a new order of clarity and awareness.

*I'm at Mom's house. She shows me old pictures; one is of Grandpa. There is a teacup full of old small things like a child's barrettes and baby pins. Mom lectures me on sexual morals. She breaks down crying. I had gone to her for help, but she couldn't cope. I say I will help her with her addiction if she will help me with mine. Then I give a loved one some writings about myself, but after the first page, I take them back.*

# "Teacup"

OCTOBER 4, 1987

## S U S A N

*Mom is showing me something very important — my childhood things in a teacup — barrettes and baby pins, and a picture of my grandfather. She is giving me clues about my childhood. The grandfather picture and the baby items are presented to me with an anguished commentary about sexual morals. It is overwhelming for her. In this dream we are both in a lot of trouble. And finally I say that I am not ready to share my story with anyone.*

## P A T R I C I A

This dream came the day after the "Surrender" dream. It is as if the act of surrender prepared for this dream, where clues are being given about Susan's childhood trauma.

The drawing is an example of the initial dream images that Susan would make and we would work from in our sessions. In this drawing Susan is a young adolescent, her hair in a ponytail. The table again appears; this time, it is what stands between the mother and daughter. The subject at hand is on the table, the teacup holding the artifacts from childhood. The mother is showing the daughter something, trying to tell her about the past, but she herself is so conflicted that she breaks down. The anguished sermon on sexual morals leads Susan to realize that the mother needs help, too, that they are somehow in this together. The decision to share her story as she knows it is an ongoing question we hold. At this point, the dream indicates that it is not yet time; it is premature to share the story, especially because she only has the "first page" of intuitive knowing and does not yet have many facts.

*T*here is a child being held against her will. *A powerful man sits in a chair and could let her go. Another man tells him the child bears the mark of the lips of Jesus on her cheek, and therefore she is a blessed one and should be set free.*

# "Against Her Will"

OCTOBER 8, 1987

## SUSAN

*At this point it is not clear to me who the man in the chair is. Another man says that I am blessed and deserve to be free. It moves me to tears to feel that I am thought blessed and deserving.*

## PATRICIA

This dream follows shortly after the dream with the mother's attempt to talk about the past and the teacup filled with objects from childhood. Now, the young child herself enters from the dream world. In a room that is stark and bare, she is being held against her will by the man in the chair. His presence has an overwhelming power over her. The drawing places him in an almost throne-like position, emphasizing his dominance. The child is not yet close enough to recognize him; she only feels his influence.

Another man who accompanies her tells the powerful man that the child has been kissed by Jesus, that she is a special and blessed child and should be set free. This man is advocating her release from the tyranny that has held her hostage. This negotiation between the powers of good and evil for the fate of the child has a deeply emotional impact on the dreamer. We both feel it as we work. Two realizations come from this dream: first, that the child-part is being held captive by some still unknown power; and secondly that someone recognizes her goodness and is working for her release.

I know that it is not unusual for a child who has been sexually abused by an adult to have the strange feeling of being somehow "chosen," special, singled out by the perpetrator. This dream, however, inverts that terrible meaning of "chosen." The child is said to have received the kiss of Jesus, a kiss of redemption, a mark of salvation. The "advocate" is working hard for the child's release.

The drawing of the room in which this plea takes place shows the barrenness of the throne-man's domain and the stark emptiness the child-part feels, cut off and isolated from the vitality and freedom of life outside, the trees and sunlight, the world of nature.

*I* am being given rhinestones, false jewels, and a dress that is not mine.

# "Rhinestones for Red"

### NOVEMBER 8, 1987

## SUSAN

*The dress is made of dark pink chiffon. My hair is in a beehive. The jewels are costume jewelry, rhinestones. The costume is from my family; they think I look good in it. But I know it is not me. I am searching for RED, and what I have here is a sanitized version of her raunchy, wild self. Her wild hair is tied up, in control; her redness is watered down to pink, and her jewels are fake. This is a disappointing situation.*

## PATRICIA

Here we see one of the variations of the dream character called RED. In this dream she is dressed in the garb of the false, impromptu self. The last three dreams have traced RED's development: from Susan's mother attempting to show her earliest childhood trauma; to being psychically held captive against her will as a young child; to a falsely constructed woman-self. Like the dream of the cracked vase, the "family" thinks she looks good. Appeased by appearances, they approve of this persona, not wanting to see beneath the glittering falseness. This persona may fool others, but the dreamer knows it is not her true self. It is a partial self constructed from objects "given" to her to hide herself and others from the truth.

This dream and the painting give us a picture of how the split-off self develops and holds herself. This rather smug-looking woman with her jaw set and her mouth clamped in a self-satisfied smirk belies the pain and humiliation that we suspect is at the heart of her story.

*T*he whole eastern sky between the trees lights up with moving
stars — very bright, intense, with lots of movement. I know this is
a celebration dream.

# "Celebration Sky"

NOVEMBER 9, 1987

## SUSAN

*This is the first truly celebrational dream. I realize that when my dreamer asks me to do the hard work — face the tragedies, feel the pain — it will also give me the reward of beauty and joy. In the dreams there seems to be a constant balance of trauma and reward. Because of this celebrational dream, I feel confident that I will not be overloaded with pain.*

*The painted image juxtaposes the red house on the right and the green house on the far left. These two opposing color energies appear in my work often; this red feels like life and passion and the green like sickness and death.*

## PATRICIA

This dream occurs in the midst of deep winter. It presents us with some grand night sky phenomena — an indication to me that the changes in awareness are being registered as cosmic in magnitude. The stars are moving, the constellations changing. Susan, the dreamer, sees this and feels it as a very positive sign. We look to the sky for signs and wonders; the movement is extraterrestrial, not of the earth. The universe is responding to this process in some deep way. The red house, the house of RED, is moving more fully into the frame as the green house of sickness is pushed out of the frame.

*A* *lover has a picture of me draped in red and black and posed like Ingres' Odalisque.*

## "The Sphinx"
### NOVEMBER 11, 1987

SUSAN
*Through the art-making process, my unconscious is informing me about the dream image. Here, my creative process transforms the dream Odalisque into a painting of The Sphinx. How does this happen?*

*As I am looking at the drawing I made of the recumbent female, I think of stripping the image down and simplifying what I see. The pose I give her is from a Matisse nude, angular and abstract. As her shape becomes more abstract she loses her personal significance and evolves into a more universal female form. Now when I feel her presence, it is clear to me that she is a being of great knowledge and wisdom.*

*For me,* Odalisque *is an image of female sexuality enslaved, while* The Sphinx *represents the silent guardian of knowledge. The presence of the sphinx indicates to me that there is a riddle to be solved. The sphinx is holding the key. In the dream there are two colors, red and black. As I made the painting the odalisque's sexual power of red became inter-twined with the sphinx's mystery of black.*

*This dream seems to be telling me I need to examine my male/female relationships and my relationship to my own sexuality. It raises questions: Where have I enslaved myself? And why? The answers lie in examining the past, in the process of remembering.*

PATRICIA

In the dream the "lover has a picture." In other words, the lover has made a certain kind of projection, a fantasy, a stereotype of female sexuality, in the form of an odalisque. As Susan points out, Ingres' painting is one of the classical images of enslaved female sexual power. An odalisque is a sexual slave, a harem concubine. She is in the painting solely as a sexual signifier, seductive, recumbent, in sexual servitude both to her master, the harem owner, and to the male artist's gaze, presented for the viewer's delectation. We do not know what she feels; we see only her inscrutable stare.

In transcribing the dream image into a painting, Susan lets the odal-isque transform herself into a sphinx. A sphinx is another classical female image — this time a signifier of female knowledge. I know that in ancient Egyptian mythology, the sphinx is the lion-headed, winged god-dess Hathor, who asks the mystical riddle and kills those who cannot answer. In Greek myth, the sphinx asks her riddle of Oedipus. When he answers the sphinx correctly, Oedipus is immediately blinded by his insight into his incestuous relations with his mother. The sphinx is often portrayed as part animal, part human, combining instinctual wisdom with female knowing. She is a divinity and is thought of as the keeper of the riddle, the silent one who holds the knowledge of life's deepest secrets. Susan's odalisque/sphinx invites her to confront her own riddles, seeking the answers to questions that still mystify her about her history and current behavior.

*Birds* come to me from over the ocean: all blue, bright, large ones and tiny white and grey spotted ones. I feel their feet on my upturned palms.

# "Thunderbirds"

## NOVEMBER 18, 1987

### SUSAN

*In the dream the tiny birds land on my outstretched palms. Their feet feel light and scratchy. I feel honored to receive them. The big, blue birds float down with their wings outstretched. They appear to just float down toward earth. This is not the flight of a regular bird. When I drew these birds in the sky over the ocean, they became schematic, like Native American Thunderbirds. The blue Thunderbirds are the color of the sky, and their red heads make them ceremonial. The thrill of the tiny, wild bird feet on my hands and the awesome visual display of the big birds in the sky make this dream feel like a blessing. My dreams are encouraging me to continue.*

### PATRICIA

The bird spirits are arriving from far away, from "over the ocean." The dreamer's open, upturned palms invite them to land, and she feels their sensate reality. She is put "in touch" with these soul-birds. Their arrival signals a fresh infusion of spiritual energy. We feel the lift they bring and are glad for their appearance.

I go back to Eliade. He notes that in most mythologies, "Birds are psychopomps." They conduct the souls to the afterworld. They can also be the souls themselves, as the birds' faculty of flight gives them access to the heavens. In this dream the birds are arriving, and the dreamer feels their arrival as a "blessing," a sign. By now we are alerted to the dreams' rhythm. Encouraging, spirit-lifting dreams are presented before and after the dreams that give clues to the trauma mystery.

*I approach the woman, Suzanna, in her bed and feel her breast. I lean to kiss her, but I have no lips. She pushes me away.*

# "Mask"

### SUSAN

*The woman in this dream and I are at odds. I am trying for intimacy but am unknowingly wearing a lipless grimace, which frightens the woman. How did this mask become a part of me? This dream feels like part of a complicated, darkly woven memory. The painting shows the color red surrounding the women, but their faces are white, drained of color like ghosts, or the dead. There is no connection between them, only the struggle of coming near and pushing away.*

### PATRICIA

We found the striking element in this dream to be the "lipless grimace," which Susan perceives as a mask. In the dream and in the painting, there is a troubled attempt to make contact. Susan's gesture toward Suzanna is erotic, sensual, desiring. Suzanna's repulsion draws attention to what is wrong — the lipless grimace — and leads us, as we work with the dream, to questions about this facial feature. The name "Suzanna" alerts us to the notion that this is some aspect of Susan, some part she is trying to get close to. The color red in the painting locates the dream's atmosphere; it is something about RED's story. We don't know what the strange "lipless grimace" is about, but the feeling is ominous and repulsive. Susan is very disturbed to feel that look on her own face and identifies it as a mask, something she has taken on. This dream with its attempted "kiss" leaves us with a threatening, sinister feeling.

*An* earthquake hits. The school building turns upside-down. I look for my dog and find him outside. There is a slight wound on his shoulder, but he is all right and glad to see me. We get cans of red paint and put them in the red wagon. The wagon belongs to my grandfather.

# "Schoolhouse Ruin"
### DECEMBER 13, 1987

## SUSAN

*My knowledge, my "schoolhouse," is thrown upside-down by uncontrollable forces. My version of reality is being destabilized. All memory, beliefs, and relationships have come into question. What has precipitated this earthquake? My guardian dog is standing by.*

## PATRICIA

As we work on this dream, we do not know, although we can feel it, that we are being moved closer to the revelation of trauma. As this dream shows, Susan experiences a great deal of upheaval during this time. The ground on which she has been standing quakes, and the little red "schoolhouse" where she has been taught how and what to think is now totally upside down. Everything is in a state of reversal; what was once thought to be true is not. This signifies the level of betrayal she is feeling. However, the appearance of her dog, a faithful companion and protector, gives us encouragement. He has sustained a slight wound in this massive upset, but he is still present, alert, and available. No one else was hurt. There is some activity at the end which entails red paint and the red wagon. From the color red, we know we are in RED's territory.

*We are preening one another. I begin to arrange her hair, and she finishes it. I am her daughter.*

# "The Combing"

## SUSAN

*This dream came on the same night as the "Schoolhouse Ruin" dream. It shows an intimate and reflective moment shared between two women. They are dressing their hair, which is a skill learned by all women, passed on from mother to daughter. The dream itself seems ordinary, but when I make images of the women the art-making process transforms them from the everyday to the mythic realm, where they become tribal women.*

*How does this transformation actually happen? My artistic sensibility tells me to make them in black ink, a simple, powerful, and beautifully rich color. Then I place them in a timeless, universal space. Stripped down to their essence, their state of being is what remains. In the creative process, it is the role of the artist to allow the artistic sensibility to roam where it will and follow intuitive decisions as they come up.*

*I feel these women are related to the first dream of women prisoners who escape to become their true tribal selves. I feel they are here to teach and support me.*

## PATRICIA

As Susan notes, combing and washing women's hair is, on the one hand, a very ordinary, everyday gesture. Yet, as her painting reveals, it can also be imbued with great symbolic and ritual meaning. I know that the fixing of hair is generally part of any woman's initiation ceremony. Sometimes, in dreams, arranging hair seems to have something to do with making a change in one's way of thinking, rearranging what comes out of one's head. I wonder if this dream may be commenting on Susan's and my relationship as we work together on the dreams. It feels as if it could also be an image of Susan's relationship with her internal mother-daughter pair. Maybe it is some combination of these two themes.

This dream, following upon the upside-down schoolhouse dream with its theme of betrayal, seems to be deepening the assignment of having to re-think everything, while the dream painting continues the supportive theme of initiation by the tribal women.

*T*here is a camp in the woods with a porch like Grandma's. A boy is sweeping away leaves. The man's face sinks into itself like a moldering potato.

# "Potato Man"

DECEMBER 22, 1987

## SUSAN

*The ghost is sitting on my grandmother's porch. His spirit is weak, shriveling, and losing power. He looks familiar to me, at first like an image of a discarded lover. Then he becomes the deflated image of my grandfather. The broom is indicating a clearing away, a clean sweep.*

 *This dream occurred at the time of my grandfather's funeral. When I attended the funeral and saw him in the casket I was confused. I never felt sad; I felt nothing. It was as though I did not know who he was. My own family looked like strangers to me. It was a reality warp like the Twilight Zone, or the schoolhouse being turned upside-down.*

## PATRICIA

The autumn leaves are being brushed away, revealing the moldering ghost of a "potato man" in the last stages of decay. In the painting he has his hands tucked into his crotch. Protectively or pointedly? Although at first there was some identification with an old lover, this is the first image that Susan clearly starts to recognize as her grandfather, her mother's father. In waking life he has recently died, and Susan has experienced a strange blankness, an emotional numbing, around this event and the funeral. From these signs, we are beginning to wonder if this grandfather was an abuser.

*Some boys are fixing up my old red sports car. Although it is barely running, the car is quite red and beautiful. They talk me into taking a test drive, even though the car is not yet legal.*

# "Test Drive"

## S U S A N

*The red sports car is mechanically shaky. It is not legal; it has no registra-*
*tion papers, no inspection. I am willing to go around the block in it.*
*Taking this car out feels like setting the lizards free and opening the gates*
*for the wild horses. I must proceed with caution. I am getting a taste of*
*freedom here, although something seems fragile and I need to take care.*

## P A T R I C I A

In a previous dream, this car was ice blue in color with nothing but RED's
clothing — the long red gloves, red dress, and red shoes — on the inside.
Now the red color is on the outside, and Susan, the dreamer, is driving.
She begins to take her partially restored vehicle for a spin around the
block, testing her newfound female energy, feeling the momentary exhila-
ration of freedom. The dream tells us that this is, however, only a test drive,
letting us know that there is more to work through. It would be premature
to take off now, thinking all was in order. The chances for trouble are still
great. This dream appears shortly after her grandfather's death, and we
wonder if it is possible that RED feels some liberation from his passing.

*A lover wants to buy me a wrap. All the clothes are sarongs, chadoras, silk wraps in beautiful colors. I am given a black one with tiny rhinestones like the night sky. I have to learn to walk without stepping on it, by kicking it up a bit. My lover becomes a woman. She wears a black sarong with a red stripe, and she is speaking passionately against my cheek.*

# "The Message"
## JANUARY 19, 1988

### SUSAN

*Her message to me is, "Your passion is your own." It belongs to no one. It is given by no one. I am free when I know this.*

*This beautiful dream is filled with feelings of erotic passion and well-being. The dream is re-collecting part of my being, returning what had been fractured and given away. There is a great and powerful reuniting with my eros, my female passion. The dream gives me this reunion as a gift.*

### PATRICIA

This dream was very moving. It gives the message that all women need to hear: "Your passion is your own." It is filled with various "wraps" made of beautiful fabrics, recalling the names of female garments from all over the world. Susan, the dreamer, is presented with one in particular, a black one with tiny rhinestones. Here the rhinestones, which in a previous dream were the "false jewels," are now like stars, the tiny sparkling lights in the black night sky. This gift involves developing some skill. She can't just take it and go; she must learn to watch her step.

When her lover becomes a woman, the dream continues the work of integrating her once split-off sexual wisdom, gifting her with her own special wrap. The lover wears a black sarong with a red stripe, combining the two colors that have been separated in previous dreams. We feel that this deeply restorative dream and its painting belong to the developing female initiation series.

73

*I take my teddy bear by the arm and slip out the back door of the house. I walk around the front corner of the garage. I feel a presence behind me. I look and see my grandfather sitting in his chair in the corner by the door. He is younger; his eyes are piercing blue and leering. He is smiling at me. I thought he was dead, but he isn't. I feel a recoiling shock in my body. My mouth opens to scream, yet no scream could come out.*

# "Grandfather"
### JANUARY 22, 1988

## SUSAN

*This is an ambush dream. It is intensely realistic. I awake, terrified, with my mouth still open in a silent scream. If Grandfather is not dead, he is still dangerous. His teeth are bared. His mouth makes a no-lip smile that is meant to reassure me, but I can feel his malevolent intention. This dream sends a recoiling shock throughout my body. I remember the same silent scream from recurring childhood nightmares.*

*With sadness I begin to realize that this is the person who has done great harm to me. I must tell someone this time. I wake my partner to tell the dream in a whispered voice. Then, I write the dream and draw the face. I saw him. I am sure.*

## PATRICIA

This dream, with its realism, emotional intensity, and fear, connects Susan immediately with her childhood nightmares. Her recognition of the grandfather brings together some elements familiar to us from other dreams. The origin of the leering, "lip-less" grin, which had appeared on Susan's face as a mask in a previous dream is now revealed. The unknown powerful man in the chair, the one who held the young child "against her will" in an earlier dream, is now recognized. In the painting of this dream, Susan gave the grandfather a shirt of sickly green and placed him on a chair of vibrant plush red. Is he the one who has been sitting on RED?

It is no surprise that Susan's dream produced this image at this time. We had been preparing for it in some way all along. It is not unusual for a woman who has been sexually traumatized as a child by someone in her family to begin to have memories after the person has died. Death seems to release something in a woman's psyche so that she can begin the process of remembering. Along with the tremendous terror Susan feels, there is a sense of relief at least in knowing who we are dealing with. In spite of her fear, she has a strong sense of confirmation.

*I am having intercourse with a man larger than me, older than me. I am detached; I just lie there and submit. A circle of boys stands around me; they judge and criticize me. I am bad. I climb to the top of the wardrobe in my grammar school looking for my jewelry boxes. I have three, and when I find them, they are all empty. My heart is broken. I had so many beautiful pieces of jewelry.*

## "The Jewel Box: Part I"
JANUARY 23, 1988

### SUSAN
*I feel depressed and sad when I wake up from this dream. The feeling of loss has lasted all day. My self-value, my jewels, have been stolen by a perpetrator's grievous act.*

# "The Jewel Box: Part II"

JANUARY 26, 1988

*A woman finds my lost wallet with money in it in the sand. She returns it to me. She also gives me back my box of stolen jewelry.*

### SUSAN

*My self-value is being restored to me in this dream. Here, a woman who is a healer is helping me rediscover my self-worth. In the painting, the women again change into tribal women. During the ritual of art-making, I channel the energy of the dream into visual images by meditating on what occurs in the dream and bringing the essence of it through my body and out onto the paper. In my experience, creating art from a dream source feels like it happens automatically, without conscious intervention. However, once the elemental nature of the dream appears on paper, it is subjected to that part of my creative process which involves critical thinking and decision making. Painting the women in the act of restoration is what transforms them from the ordinary to the sacred. This dream helps me feel like I am beginning to reclaim my self-esteem.*

### PATRICIA

These two dreams coming three days apart show us, in a very condensed visual and metaphorical way, the tremendous feelings of loss and grief that accompany sexual trauma, followed by the blessings of restoration and reward that are potentially available in a therapeutic process.

In the first dream Susan feels and sees the results of her childhood trauma; when she has intercourse with an older, larger man, she becomes submissive and detached. She sees a woman disassociated from her sexuality, a woman disconnected from her sexual experience, who is subject to the taunting, judging criticism of a collection of immature masculine energies. In an effort to restore her sense of self-worth, she goes back to her grammar school to retrieve something she has left there, something from her childhood, hidden away at the top of the wardrobe. There is a feeling that she knows, she remembers, she once had something precious. But now, in the dream search, she finds her three jewelry boxes are empty, the jewels gone, stolen, disappeared.

This dream produces very strong feelings of sadness and loss. There is a sense of deep mourning and grief for what has been wrongfully taken. She sees that something precious once belonged to her; now, it has been stolen. She feels the violation of being robbed. In this way, the dream is helping with her bereavement. Despite its painful message and the haunting feeling of loss, this is an important part of the healing process.

In the following dream a woman finds Susan's lost wallet. She returns it along with her lost jewelry box. The wallet, an image of identity, has been found in the sand. Has it washed up from the sea of the unconscious? It still contains money; her self-worth is intact. A box of stolen jewelry is also restored to her by this woman, whom Susan identifies as a healer. In this dream, the archetype of healer has been constellated — one who heals by returning to Susan what has always been hers, her ego identity along with its currency, as well as the deeper soul treasures.

The dream is mirroring our process, as well as raising Susan's own inner healer. This dream provides us with an empowering and reassuring image, giving a necessary feeling of inner strength.

I notice that in the prior dream, there were three jewel boxes. Yet, only one has been returned. Where are the other two? Will they come back to her as well? Or has something been irretrievably lost?

*I eat a cream-filled pastry. It squirts into my mouth and plops down on my chest. I feel humiliated.*

# "Exploding Eclair"

JANUARY 27, 1988

SUSAN

*The feeling of humiliation tells me something bad is happening. I feel vulnerable and victimized.*

PATRICIA

This dream, with its visceral sensations and feelings of mortification, is clearly linked with the sexual abuse trauma. Susan's painting is graphic. The girl's eyes register the shock; she is dressed in the ice-blue color of numbness; the background wallpaper is red, chaotic with scattered dots and stains.

*A girl drops her head, opens her mouth, and drools onto the table. At first I think it is a joke, and she is going to laugh. But she looks up and wails in terror. Everything is in slow motion, black and white. Her mouth opens wide, and she screams, "MOMMY." The mother stands up and in the same terror screams her daughter's name. The father stands up and says, "What is going on?" A car I drive is going faster and faster. It has lost its brakes and will crash at the end of the road. My wisdom tooth falls out.*

# "Grief"

JANUARY 28, 1988

## SUSAN

*I am moving at breakneck speed toward some great terror. The grief and horror of the little girl evoke for me that haunting picture from Vietnam of the screaming naked child running down the road away from her napalmed village.*

*In the dream, the girl's painful wail is heard and felt by the mother. The father is trying to understand what is happening. The family is my family.*

## PATRICIA

Within a one-week period, Susan is flooded with trauma dreams as the process of remembering intensifies. The sensation of a speeding car with no brakes gives the accurate feel. There are literally "no breaks" right now. These dreams are filled with terror and humiliation; the images are telling us what has happened as well as connecting Susan with the powerful emotions associated with her childhood trauma. In the dream the mother responds in a completely empathic way. All violated daughters desperately need and desire a fiercely feeling, responding mother. Although Susan has yet to actually tell her own mother what she remembers, we know that the dream mother has been in this story from the beginning. The father in the dream is bewildered by the intensity of emotion coming from this mother/daughter pair.

Although the background in the painting is very dark, Susan places a lit candle next to the terrorized girl. The light of the soul's awareness is still burning.

*I take a vacation to Bloomingdale's. The store becomes full of poor, black women. They put on black and red dresses; everyone wears jet jewelry. We all join hands in a circle to sing and dance. I wear all black.*

# "Dancers"
## JANUARY 29, 1988

## SUSAN

*The tribal women return to my dreams. We are transformed by joy and companionship. Wearing the dresses and jewels marks an honoring and celebration of ourselves. It is a relief and a respite from last week's dreams of terror.*

## PATRICIA

This dream echoes the first dream with the poor black women on the train. This time the women are donning the black and red dresses that we now recognize as a sign of psychic integration. The black — of deep night, the unconscious, grief — is paired with red — the color of passion, sexuality, life. Susan wears all black; her initiation is still in progress.

This vacation/celebration following the wrenching trauma dreams offers us an inbreath, a blessed relief, a needed break from the hard work of remembering — as well as the reassurance that the deeper levels of healing are indeed occurring.

*I* take off my shoes and walk over an isthmus; I am wearing black stockings. I get on a wagon pulled by a horse which enters a high rolling sea. The destination is far off. The woman driver tells me that the horse has never swum the ocean before. It's a scary ride.

# "Crossing"

FEBRUARY 7, 1988

## S U S A N

*The waves are big, and the horse is working very hard. We have such a long way to go. I am not sure the horse will have enough strength to make the crossing. This dream feels like the crocodile ride; only here, I have more than just a tail to hang onto. I have the horse and a driver to take me there. I make a decision to hold on and go for it. This dream is telling me that I still have a long way to go in my recovery process. It is also giving me assistance in the form of horse power and a guide.*

## P A T R I C I A

In this dream Susan is still wearing black — left over from the last dream. She has taken her shoes off, becoming *discalced* — a term used for religious orders who do not wear shoes. In myth, those entering the underworld are not shod; they do not wear the shoes of the everyday world, their earthly walk. So these few details alert us to another period of deepening. An isthmus is a narrow strip of land that runs between two bodies of water. The earth world is narrowing and Susan enters again into the depths of the unconscious. She makes a decision to step onto the horse-drawn wagon. She is aware of the dangers, the high seas, the fact that the horse is working hard. She is given no guarantees of safety; in fact, she is told that the horse has never swum in the ocean before. There is risk; it will be a difficult passage.

This dream echoes the earlier "Guardians" dream of the nightsea journey. Yet it feels different this time. The slow, silent, inevitability is replaced with a heightened awareness of how risky and strenuous the journey is. The forces of the ocean are powerful; the horse is inexperienced; the distance is far. There is no easy comfort given to either of us, no naive reassurances. One cannot be gullible or innocent when undertaking such a journey; one can only be aware of the potential risks and gains and make a choice.

In many ways, Susan and I came upon this choice-point many times. It was as if the dreams gave her the opportunity, time and again, to say yes to the process. Yes, we will proceed. Yes, we will go deeper. I take the "woman driver" in the dream to be about both my role in the process — my task of guidance through the turbulent waters, as well as my own unknowing — and Susan's inner guide, her inner wisdom.

*I* have an environmental art show at my gallery. Drawings are on the walls and ceiling.

# "Dream Interior"

FEBRUARY 8, 1988

## SUSAN

*I am enveloped in the dream space; it feels like looking out from the dream's interior. The space is rich and comfortable, beautifully painted and dark. There is a shining light on the outside. Here, I am stepping back looking at myself in this mysterious process, surrounded by images from my unconscious.*

## PATRICIA

This was one of those deeply mysterious dreams that make one wonder if the ancient mystics are not right — that we are all simply dreaming ourselves, that our lives are merely our deepest meditative dreams. The dream and the painting have a strong sense of inner and outer space. The inside is rich and dark and full of images, like a cave, while the outside is bright and full of shining light. Are we given, in this dream, not only an image of the unconscious and the conscious, but also a sense of the rich, embodied life with all its varied images and the light of pure spirit, what we go toward when we die? In any case, in this dream, Susan is located, deeply enveloped, in the dream world space. It is her "environment," the source of her life and her art.

This dream stands in sharp contrast to the earlier dream where the child is held hostage by a tyrannical man in the barren room. In that dream there was also the sense of an inner and outer space — the inside being the isolated, sequestered life of the little girl's trauma, the outside an unavailable world filled with life and vitality. Here, Susan is located deeply within herself, within the creative, fecund world of images which faces out toward the light.

*These are caves from an ancient time. Women are in them. The caves are long, narrow, and connected. One must crawl through them. One woman is a powerful oracle who sees many things. She is speaking of "the son of woman" and how he must change. The cave has an opening to the starry night sky.*

# "The Cave"

## FEBRUARY 8, 1988

### SUSAN

*Emerging from the cave feels like a birthing process. The cave is the body of the earth. The opening in the earth's body shows the starry night sky of the outer world. The figure is bald, like an infant or priestess. The male pictogram with the lightning bolt sends a message from the ancient past. I take this dream as a recognition of my personal and cultural wounding by our patriarchal society. I recognize a deep knowing by women that it must all change.*

### PATRICIA

This dream occurred on the same night that Susan dreamed of the dream interior. It feels like a very deep and powerful dream, pulled from the depths of what Jung called the collective unconscious. The previous dream located Susan in the deep interior of the dream space. In this dream she is being taken back to the caves, the earliest known ritual space, where images were made on walls by our Paleolithic ancestors. The cave has always been recognized as an analog for the womb, and in early human times, as a place for sacred rites and initiations where spiritual knowledge was received and recorded. This dream has an awesome quality, as if we are being told about something critically important. The female oracle/priestess with her prophetic message about "the son of woman" — not the Christian "son of man" — must be a collective message for our time.

The act of returning to the womb/cave for spiritual knowledge and the rebirth of wisdom must be a deeply embedded human impulse. The painting puts the bald and naked woman in the birth canal; the night sky is visible through the opening, and she is heading toward it. This inner and outer space is echoed again from the previous dreams.

The pictogram on the wall is reminiscent of ancient rock art. The image is a spirit catcher, a human or a shaman in the shape of a thunderbird. His head is red and there is a lightning bolt at his head, signifying either knowledge or enlightenment being received or an energy charge and knowledge being transmitted out. We are greatly awed and energized by this dream.

*Five women are in the desert. I walk over to one and say, "I have seen you before in dreams." She says, "Yes, you have."*

# "Desert Goddess"

FEBRUARY 14, 1988

## SUSAN

*In the dream the women are making a golf course out of the desert with their hands. This is amazing to me. They have the power to create fertility where none had existed before. The "Queen of the Night" is among the women. It is She that I have seen before.*

*I feel I am put back in touch with my creative powers here. I am being shown that one can create fertile land in seemingly barren spaces. This seems to be saying something about the dreaming, art-making process, where my creative efforts are yielding new growth. The reappearance of the "Queen of the Night" with the creating women tells me my dream guardians and guides are interrelated and familiar with one another. I feel encouraged and happy.*

## PATRICIA

This feeling of familiarity is very comforting at a time when things have gotten so "hot." Even the dream's play on the desert, a hot and seemingly barren place, is reassuring in that it offers continuity and coherence with the previous dream's indication that things are heating up. The idea that these women are making a golf course out of the desert by hand tells us that there is a transformation in progress. It is done slowly, but intentionally. The miracle of green on a desert landscape is not something that nature provides; it must come from careful and purposeful labor. The recognition of the dream figure by the dreamer and the mutual acknowledgement of familiarity by the "Desert Goddess" give us a deeply felt comfort and awareness.

*I am looking at my boat. It is unpainted, neglected. A man wants to chop it up for kindling. I say, "No, we must fix her up." When we do, she floats, although she is in rough shape.*

# "Voyager"

## SUSAN

*I don't want to give up this boat. It may be in tough shape, but it is worth saving. In this dream the boat is like the red sports car — shaky but salvageable. In some dreams, the boat takes me into circumstances that are difficult, or scary, like a waterfall or a typhoon. In other dreams, I will be sailing along with a good wind into a dark and mysterious place. To me, the boat follows the path my spirit is taking. If I pay attention, it will tell me what course I am headed on.*

## PATRICIA

As a vehicle that can ride the seas, the boat mediates between the dreamer and the unconscious deeps. In this dream the boat appears to be in jeopardy. To be in working order, a boat like this needs to be maintained. In the dream, however, it has been left neglected. A decision has to be made: Susan's masculine side says chop it up, but her feminine dream-ego decides to make the necessary repairs. This dream and the image Susan paints show an upright woman steering her course. Susan made her into one of the tribal women, so we know that this is part of the female tribal initiation series. From the dream we also know that the boat, although she can float, is still in need of work. We suspect she will not have smooth sailing for awhile.

*I am washing the hair of a woman. Her hair is long, thick, and curly. I ask her to be patient since I haven't done much hairdressing.*

# "The Washing"

FEBRUARY 22, 1988

## SUSAN

*These are ordinary women in the dream, but when I make the images of them, they become archetypal, tribal women. The hairwashing feels ritualistic, like the previous dream of combing. It is a service one woman performs for another. Here, the washing ceremony is a cleansing. I make the bowl red to reflect its special importance. I am cleansing away sorrow, regrets, and pain.*

## PATRICIA

This dream sends us back to the earlier dream "The Combing," where Susan is also the hairdresser. Here, she acknowledges her inexperience and asks for patience. There is a sense of mutuality in this activity. She is performing this ritual cleansing on another woman whose hair is thick and curly. Vibrant hair is thought to be a sign of health and beauty. To be "in service" to this woman with the luxuriant hair is to be in a position of ritual attendance. The relationship is one of assistance and honoring while maintaining one's own dignity and power. There is also a sense of preparation that we feel from this dream.

*I bite off a penis. I have it in my mouth. I have held it in there for a long time. It is disgusting. I spit it out into my hand in pieces.*

# "Purple Hearts"

MARCH 22, 1988

## SUSAN

*This is one of the saddest and most painful dreams I have ever had. It is difficult for me to write about it even now. The child's putrid green skin shows how sick she is feeling. It is indescribably horrible to cough up such a terrible and secret wounding. The expectorated pieces have the consistency of cooked organs, which is why I call this piece "Purple Hearts." Everyone recognizes the purple heart as the badge of the battle-wounded.*

## PATRICIA

This dream stunned us with its blatant imagery. As sad and painful as it is, the dream gives us further confirmation of both the events that we are trying to recover and the healing direction of the dream world. This dream graphically shows us how abuse becomes incorporated, taken in by the child and held for many years, both as a secret and as a source of "sickness." To expel these undigested bits, this "foreign" body part, is to externalize the trauma, getting it up and out, out of the body memory, and out of its sequestered place in the psyche. Here, as the painting shows, it is in hand, visible, seen. It is as if the source of decay which had caused the earlier dream with the maggots is now spit out.

Susan paints the face in this painting as sick a color green as she could find. The painting and the color green are representations of both the thing that made her sick and the results of her sickness. She titles the dream "Purple Hearts" because what she has in her hand looks like that and because a "Purple Heart" is a badge awarded to those who have been wounded and survive. Despite the anguish, there is a certain amount of relief that accompanies our work on this dream. At least it is out.

*I*n a play, Scarlett O'Hara is playing Scarlett O'Hara. The actress takes off her bonnet and jacket when she sees the real Scarlett O'Hara and sings, "I Feel Pretty." They embrace, compliment, and validate each other.

# "Scarlett O'Hara Meets Scarlett O'Hara"

MARCH 27, 1988

## SUSAN

*The two women recognize and value one another. Scarlett/RED is embracing the other Scarlett/RED. This feels like a welcoming home after a long period of separation. It is a joyful occasion, to see and accept and love oneself.*

## PATRICIA

It is comforting to know that the dream world has a sense of humor and is witty, that it likes to play with words and images, making puns and double entendres. This single dream image plays on many themes that have been present throughout the earlier dreams. This dream reminds us of other dreams where parts of the self are met and mirrored — for instance, the dream where Susan reached out for Suzanna. In that dream there was a traumatized feminine energy longing for connection. This dream is also a further development of the dream "Rhinestones for Red," where RED's impromptu persona was all dressed up in a false self. In this dream we know for certain that Scarlett is RED and O'Hara is a play on the word hair, which has been one of the important symbols in the dream series. In *Gone With the Wind*, Scarlett O'Hara is a heroine who has endured and matured through the ordeals of civil war, and as a character she has a high sense of self-esteem. In Susan's dream Scarlett O'Hara is singing "I Feel Pretty," a song meant to convey feelings of feminine self-confidence. This dream meeting and mirroring signals a kind of fusion; the actress, Scarlett O'Hara, is playing herself. There is no split here between the real self and the false self. The embrace of the two parts gives us a feeling that there is self-recognition, value, and self-appreciation. Coming after the "Purple Hearts" dream, it shows us how the dream world is self-correcting and self-healing. Once the pain of the abuse has been spit up, the feminine psyche begins to be restored to its original feelings of vibrancy and beauty.

*M*y *grandfather walks by me and pinches my breast. I grab him by the neck and threaten him. I say, "Don't you ever touch me like that again!" He pushes a girl down over the table and lies over her. I pull him off and threaten him with my fist and say, "Don't you touch her!!" Some family members think he is being cute, and I am overreacting. My grandmother comes in and says he didn't mean to harm the children.*

# "Warrior Child"

MARCH 29, 1988

## SUSAN

*At last I have found my voice! I will fight back when someone tries to victimize me. Finally, I have worked through the pain enough to find my power. It was necessary to go back, to remember, to feel, to mourn, in order to move ahead and become unstuck from the cycle of abuse.*

*In the painting I made, the image of the child is in red paint. She is a young version of RED, and a powerful, angry one. The grandfather image is putrid green for the sickness he has. He is losing power. I felt really BIG after this dream.*

## PATRICIA

This dream and the painting Susan made from it are very empowering. Following "Purple Hearts," Susan met and recognized her "beautiful" self as the heroine Scarlett O'Hara. After claiming her womanly beauty, she is now, in this dream, able to defend it. In the painting Susan makes the image of her defender in the body of a child, but the child is not weak or vulnerable; rather, she is as big as the abuser and more powerful. It is very important that Susan feel the protective energy and power of the "Warrior Child." We can sense that this feeling of power will translate into her waking life whenever she will need to call on it. The denial and the refusal of some family members to see and acknowledge the abuse let us know why the child was not protected from the perpetrator in the first place and that future confrontations with these family members, although necessary, may not be easy.

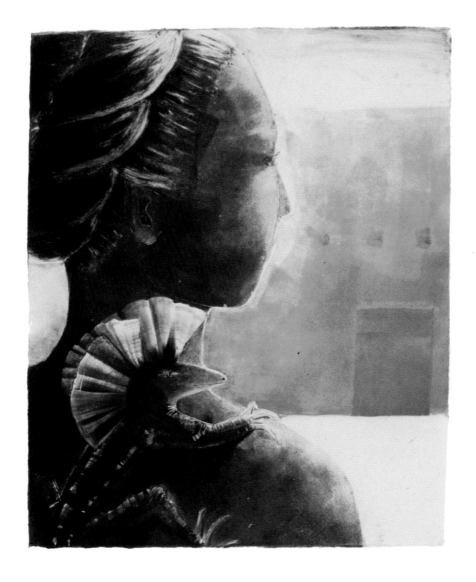

*We are playing lizard games on a street in Europe. The lizards are running up over our backs, and we are herding them with our feet.*

# "Lizard Games"

APRIL 16, 1988

## SUSAN

*The lizard is riding my shoulder as a guardian. I recognize this type of lizard. It has a comb it raises when attacked so that it can't be eaten. The presence of these lizards lets me know that I now carry a much improved radar and protection system. As a wounded woman, I was an easy prey; as a whole woman, I am becoming strong and aware.*

## PATRICIA

This dream and the image Susan painted continue the lizard theme that emerged in earlier dreams. The previous lizards were breaking out of the container where they had been boxed up. There were many of them, indicating a kind of collective liveliness needing to be let loose. In this dream they are free. This energy "running up over our backs" could be like the release of kundalini energy in the spine — and an energizing result of the previous dream's powerful confrontation. In the painting the protective, instinctual energy takes the form of this particular kind of lizard spirit. It sits on her shoulder, close to her ear so she can hear its wisdom. Susan now has direct contact with this representation from the reptilian brain, the part of the brain that is concerned with survival. It is her early warning system.

*The sea is engulfing our ocean-front camp. Green water and seaweed are flowing by the bedroom window. Outside, chairs and beds are washing back and forth. My family is inside the house. The house stands sound.*

# "Awash"

## SUSAN

*A catastrophic event is happening outside, but we are safe inside. Our little house stands on solid ground, and my family is with me. This dream is telling me that a major flood of information is immanent. I am protected by my safe, solid ground, with people around who love me. So I am prepared for what is to come.*

### PATRICIA

Big water dreams are, as Susan says, dreams of flooding, usually very emotional in nature. The feeling of being overwhelmed by water that has breached its banks is similar to the feeling of being overcome with feelings, particularly watery emotions — tears, grief, sorrow. Big water washes away; it is part of a process of dissolving, taking things back into their original element of water. In this dream the water has reached the flood mark; the house is completely submerged. Yet it is not being swept away. This dream gives Susan a feeling of groundedness in the midst of tremendous emotional inundation. Her structure is solid enough to withstand whatever is to come. This dream lets us know that there is, indeed, more to come and that she will be able to handle it.

# "Violent Intention"

## APRIL 22, 1988

*T*here is a birthday party at grand-ma's house. Everyone is there — Aunt and Uncle, kids, Mom and Dad, and me. Somehow I start saying everything that happened to me as a child. When I am finished, people act alienated. I want to know what I said. I blacked out while I spoke and couldn't remember what I said. "What did I say?" I ask Mom. "What did I say?" I ask Dad. No one would tell me. We back Great-Uncle's car to the barn, we are all in it. I want to call Patricia from a phone booth. I say to them, "I know where all the pieces are, and if I find them you have to tell me

what I said." I go outside and dig under the driveway with a trowel. I find all the broken pieces of a blue and white bowl. I find all the pieces together, and they form a whole. I say to them, "Now you have to tell me!" "I want you to bring Grandpa back alive." They do not want to. "Yes," I demand. Grandma gets a hypodermic needle and injects him. He is alive! He is

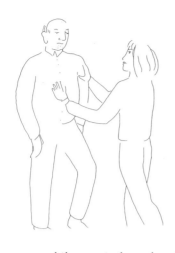

walking away from me. I walk in front of him, stepping backwards, asking questions. "Did you touch me?" I want to know. He walks and looks away. "Did you touch me?" I repeat. "Yes," he admits. "And what about the blow job. Was there a blow job?" "Yes," he says, continuing to walk away. I have a body memory of being pressed back and down against something cold and smooth, an automobile or window glass. Then I feel pebbles and small cuts in my back. The dream says that he is a failure as a singer/salesman/performer. Then I ask him, "Did you love me?" He looks right at me and says, "Yes, I did." I cry. His body falls apart in decay.

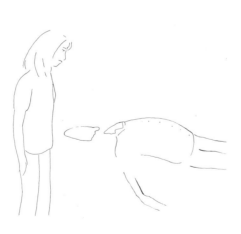

# SUSAN

*This is such a big dream, I hardly know where to begin to talk about it. The overwhelming feeling I get is confirmation that what I felt happened to me is true. Here is my evidence. I have all the pieces of the story, and a confession from the perpetrator, who was my beloved grandfather. In this dream I am able to speak to him in my adult voice, extracting the truth from him. My family is aiding me; Grandmother and Mother are on my side. The sad, sad truth of things is that Grandfather really did love me, and could hurt me in this way. I loved him, too. That is why it is so painful. Here is where I learned that relationships become destructive when love and betrayal are linked together.*

*In this dream the black hole of not-remembering is filled in. I have come to a point where the remembering will help, not harm me. A body memory is delivered back to me; in it I am feeling the entrapment and helplessness of a small, captured child. I could feel the pressure and weight of someone squishing me, causing pebbles to cut into my back. The dream says, "He is a failure as a performer." It is my sense that the violent act of rape was not completed, although the horror and intention of it was fully delivered.*

*The bowl I find is my restored spirit bowl. This dream image brings a deep soul healing, one in which I have found all the missing pieces of my life's story. I can now live with the full knowledge of my story. Through this remembering, I have been able to vent rage and sadness, and I can better understand my fears and idiosyncrasies. The overall feeling I have now is of being at peace, at rest. I have regained my power and my voice. I have found a new sense of wholeness.*

This long and complex dream comes after we have been working together for a little over a year. It is one of the most profound dreams that we work on. We are both moved by it, filled with deep awe and emotion at the dream world's precision as it moves Susan through the stages of self-recovery. All the previous dreams have prepared us, moving us forward to this point. When it comes, we are greatly relieved for many reasons, but most especially for its healing image of the spirit bowl.

One question that plagues a survivor of childhood sexual abuse is, How can one trust one's memories? Trauma frequently exists as a blank space, a "black hole," a gap in memory. This dream lets us know in no uncertain terms that we have "all the pieces." After this dream Susan and I have no doubts in our minds that all of this was true. The dream is filled with deep feeling and bodily sensations that give it an added sense of reality.

The series of drawings are what we worked from, the paintings came much later.

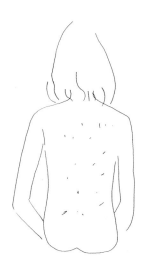

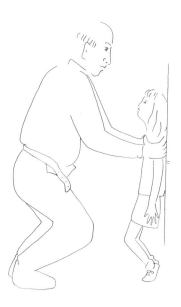

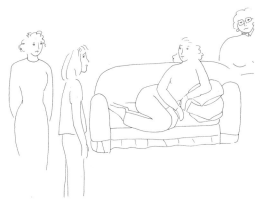

*M*om is on the couch. Sister and I are talking with her. Grandma is there. Mom says, "Grandpa was so kind; he never hurt me." I say, "Well, he hurt me bad!! He sexually assaulted me!" She looks at me in shock. Sister backs away.

I am in a store with a friend picking out graduation suits. We are choosing between the red or white with glitters. We walk out of the store wearing them, and I don't even think of paying.

# "A Graduation"

## APRIL 29, 1988

### SUSAN

*I have already paid!! I am graduating from this school of remembering. When others question or deny my story, I am confident now in my own truth. The issue of wearing red or white is interesting to me. I am choosing the white; my friend wears the red. It seems hard to decide which one I want.*

### PATRICIA

With her own truth, Susan counters her internal mother's lack of awareness. This time the sister is there, too, although she does not move toward the dreamer in support. Rather, she backs away from the dreamer's announcement of abuse. All the female family members are present here as the dreamer breaks her silence about the childhood abuse and the grandfather's actions.

The dream-healing that is taking place on an inner psychic level for Susan is also happening in Susan's outer life. We become students of the dreams' timing as the dreams show us exactly how and when she should proceed with the necessary task of speaking out to the important people in her life. Some of the encounters, like this one, are done first in the dreams. They help her prepare for the ones she will make later in waking life. These dreams give us an opportunity in our work together to strategize and begin to imagine how the confrontations would be made. The dreams' energy for truth-telling gives us energy for the work.

The second part of the dream indicates that there will be a completion to this process, a time of graduation, a marker of a task accomplished. This time Susan is with a "friend," a woman who is a "friend" to this process. This is also the first time that the color white appears as a choice. The usual colors of red and black are now joined by a powerful third color, white. This is not the white of innocence, but rather the virginal white of spirit. The colors red, black, and white are basic, archetypal — birth, death, and rebirth. As such, they belong together in the great cycle of transformation. The addition of white as a choice in this dream signifies the fulfillment of the trinity of colors. It suggests the possibility of achievement, of an inviolate wholeness.

*We walk by a pond with ducklings on top and crocodiles underneath. Every now and then, the crocodiles rise and eat one.*

# "Sitting Duck"

### MAY 29, 1988

## SUSAN

*Poor ducklings, unaware! In other dreams, the reptiles were caged in boxes;
now, they are loose and dangerous. They are what they are — carnivores.
It is the responsibility of the duck to look for one coming. A "sitting duck"
seems comical because of its lack of knowing. We can see what is about to
happen, but the duck is unaware.*

*As a child, I was young and vulnerable, like the duckling. When I
became older, I was still vulnerable because my intuitive senses were
damaged by a destructive, conflictual experience — that someone who
loves me can intentionally harm me. I could no longer trust the feelings
that told me how to recognize a person with bad intentions. Through the
recovery process, it seems possible to reclaim my intuitive knowing.*

## PATRICIA

Although this image is quite menacing, we find it also has some humor.
The "sitting duck" seems an apt image for the kind of naivete and innocence that have no concept of the dark forces hidden in the depths. In
fact, it seems that a certain kind of innocence or unconsciousness actually
draws out the crocodile in some way. A "sitting duck" is, in fact, an
unknowing, defenseless target. Throughout this process, these childlike
attitudes have been forced into a different kind of realization. The innocent trust that rightfully belongs to the child and was terribly violated and
betrayed by the abuser must give way to a deeper, more mature trust in
one's own judgments and knowing. On one level, following the dream of
"Graduation," we feel this dream is warning us not to move too quickly or
easily into a false sense of complacency. I feel that on another level, this
dream is a generalized comment about childhood sexual abuse within our
culture. There are, indeed, crocodiles in the water, and unfortunately,
children are many times "sitting ducks." The perspective of the painting
reveals both predator and prey in the same frame. For the conscious viewer,
it is an image of holistic awareness.

*There is an elephant parade. I ride the first elephant and carry a lighted candle and a spear. The elephant rises on its hind legs and puts me at the top of the evergreen tree to light the lights. The other elephants raise their forelegs onto one another's backs and form a chain.*

# "Elephant Parade"

## JUNE 5, 1988

### SUSAN

*"I know we have elephants" is a phrase from a very early dream. We were at war in that sequence, and the elephants were my allies. Here, the elephants join with me in a celebration of light. I am also carrying the spear. It feels like a victory celebration. This dream is recognizing and honoring battles accomplished. It is part of the dreams' repeated rhythm of challenge and reward. The dreams' rhythm moves the process along for me and is my incentive to continue.*

### PATRICIA

Following the dream of the predatory crocodile from the unconscious deeps, this dream gives us an image of an equally powerful force in the topside world. The elephants reappear from an earlier dream where they were part of a defense against an invasion. We have to consider the possibility that this might also be the case in this dream, a warning that another invasion of information is in the works. For the moment, however, Susan is riding on the elephant, holding a spear and a candle.

This dream is in contrast to the preceding dream where the relationship was one of predator and prey. Here, the elephant has become her sacred vehicle; she rides upon her power. The elephant is part of her, and she is part of it. They are in right and cooperative relationship with each other. The spear is her protection, as is the candle, the light of awareness. This dream image appears to be drawn from the Hindu tradition where gods and goddesses mount and ride their sacred animals, carrying implements of power and consciousness. The placing of lights on the evergreen tree comes from another ancient tradition, the festival of lights. In combination they represent a focus of energy, a commemoration of victory. The huge animals are linked together, intensifying their show of strength while demonstrating their ability to cooperate as a group.

We were thrilled and encouraged by this dream of victory and celebration. Yet, our experience tells us that after an archetypal dream of this magnitude, we must be ready for another challenge on the personal level of the trauma.

*I am looking for a civil liberties lawyer. I am very afraid. I know some-one is coming after me. I hold hands with others and meditate. The circle is broken by a pair of hands pulling me out. I turn into a small, naked child. I feel vulnerable and terrified. I try to scream — a long string of mucus comes from my throat; it tastes and looks like ejaculation. When it is out, I scream and cry. I keep hearing a child's song, "The Wheels on the Bus Go Round and Round."*

# "Civil Rights"

### JUNE 18, 1988

## S U S A N

*I am not so easily freed from my terrors. Hands are pulling me back to that place of terrible trauma. Why does this event occur now, in this dream? Why does the great dreamer think I need another reminder? I believe fear is causing this dream, the fear of retribution for truth-telling. Someone or something is trying to deny my civil right to speak out.*

## P A T R I C I A

Again, we are plunged back into the world of trauma. At this time, in her waking life, Susan is considering breaking her silence and talking to her family. The feelings about this seem to activate the trauma level again. In the dream she feels fear and is seeking an advocate, a civil liberties lawyer, to help protect and defend her rights to free speech. After the great dreams of triumph comes this dream of the child's sensation of extreme vulnerability and danger. She is being plucked out of the circle of focused meditative power by unknown hands. She opens her mouth to scream, but her throat is blocked by the physical residue of the abuse. Once it has been released, her scream and cry can be heard. The child's song is also a residue of the trauma, a trance-like song that indicates a child's way of disassociating from the abuse.

*I* *have a small boy on my lap, a baby cousin. We are sitting around a table with my grandparents. I realize that this boy has been molested by my grandfather. I press Grandfather's hand to the ground and break all of his fingers.*

# "Punishment"

JULY 2, 1988

## S U S A N

*I am relating to my grandfather on an adult level here. I am no longer stuck in a child's relationship with him. This is the first dream where I physically punish him for hurting me and others. I consider this a big step in claiming power. I am enraged when I punish him and feel I will suffer this rage for quite a while.*

## P A T R I C I A

This dream shows Susan in a protector/defender position. Here, she is no longer the helpless victim. Her energies are directed toward protection of the child and punishment and retribution for the abuser.

One of the most empowering things an abuse survivor can do is participate in a process of seeking out justice. Just as in the prior dream where Susan is looking for a lawyer, she now becomes her own prosecutor, meting out her own brand of justice. In the dream, she takes matters literally into her own hands by breaking the objects of torture. Grandfather's fingers are now unusable, no longer able to perpetrate their wrongdoings on another innocent child. These dreams express a primitive form of retribution and, although violent in that way, are extremely satisfying. The perpetrator, who is dead now in waking life, is still subject to punishment for his crimes. There is a sense of justice being meted out.

*An old black wise woman invites me to announce the heavyweight championship fight. I rush to get ready. I have a difficult time choosing my clothes. First, I try the red dress of Mom's. It doesn't fit, and I don't like it. Then, I try on the black and gold one. I am fifteen minutes late and will miss the introduction. The wise woman says, "This is the chance of a lifetime; don't miss it." I see another woman wrapped in vines and flowers, wearing a Greek dress. She is beginning the announcement. She has tremendous grace and style.*

# "One Who Speaks"

JULY 15, 1988

## SUSAN

*This is my big opportunity to speak, but I can't find a garment that defines how I feel. I am confused. The woman who goes before me carries the power of communication. She opens the way for me to speak. In waking life, when I have something very important to say, something painful or difficult, I call on her. With the help of the "One Who Speaks," my child's voice is heard.*

## PATRICIA

The "heavyweight championship fight" lets us know that there is a tremendous contest about to take place. Susan is invited to announce it, and although she readily accepts the invitation, she has some trouble preparing for it. What to wear? What persona can she call on? She cannot fit into her mother's style of presentation, and furthermore, she doesn't even like it. She finds a black and gold dress which is right, but now she has been delayed. There is great psychic pressure being brought to bear on her. There is an opportunity that can't be missed, yet there is a need to properly prepare. The dreamer is urged on by the older wise woman. Yet she still needs help. The dream provides it with the figure of a woman with ancient female roots, wrapped in vines and flowers. The Greek tunic gives her the additional attribute of a Greek goddess. She appears to be the archetypal embodiment of female speech, the one who announces the contest between truth and lies. In waking life Susan is just beginning to find her voice on these matters; she is preparing to speak out. This woman leads the way. Her voice is big and loud and clear.

*I am in a room with Grandma. Grandpa is in the background. Grandma is leaving. I go to her and kiss her cheek. I hold that kiss for a moment. She knows that it means I still love her and have separated her in my mind from my grandfather.*

# "Forgiveness"
AUGUST 2, 1988

## SUSAN

*It is important for me at this time to differentiate my grandparents from one another. I don't want to hold one responsible for the actions of the other. In the dream "Violent Intention," Grandmother assisted me in getting the truth out of Grandfather. I am letting her know that I do not blame her, and that I love her.*

## PATRICIA

*Susan's grandmother is still living. In the process of truth-telling, we plan how she will tell her grandmother what has occurred. It is important that she distinguish between the guilt of commission by the grandfather and the act of omission by the grandmother. She does not want to cut off the possibility of love. The kiss, which is held for a moment, has a dual message. A kiss can be an expression of love and a sign of betrayal. In this dream the kiss is a necessary communication, an expression of the love Susan wants to preserve. But a kiss can also contain an opposite meaning. The kiss of Jesus in an earlier dream, which marked the child as blessed is recalled. For Susan, whose child-self had once been betrayed by this woman's ignorance, it is a return of the Judas kiss, a cancelling out of the act of betrayal by an act of love.*

*I am in the desert. A man who is quiet and beautiful lives here. His aura is peaceful. I think he will teach me to ride his horse, but we talk instead. We are very intimate. When I want to leave and get some fruit, he offers me two pears. I feel a strong emotional intimacy and a conflicting need to depart. I do not want to create a physical relationship. When I leave, he follows me. Now, I am daydreaming of him and that beautiful place. Enraptured, I awake in the dream, dreaming of where I am.*

# "Desert Pears"
## SEPTEMBER 21, 1988

### SUSAN
*In this dream the light in the desert is clear and beautiful, and the house is spare and clean. I am drawn to the desert man, but experience a conflict between emotional and physical intimacy. The pears he offers are for our refreshment. I know we will eat them after we have made love. Inside this dream I daydream, then I awake, dreaming of where I am.*

### PATRICIA
We feel the spiritual energy emanating from this dream; it is palpable. The desert landscape from a previous dream appears again. The desert that had been transformed into a golf course by women who were working by hand emerges now as the home of a desert man. The masculine energy that lives in the desert is calm, quiet, intimate. The dreamer thinks she will learn how to ride a horse, that he will teach her something about coming into relationship with her powers of sexuality. Instead they talk, and he makes an offering of fruit, which the dreamer has difficulty accepting because of her ambivalence about sexual intimacy. There is no coercion or seduction here, however, only quiet invitation and an offer of shared fruit.

Like the dream and the painting "Dream Interior," this dream comments on the dreaming state, while the painting gives us a sense of inner and outer space. The perspective is again from the inside, as in the previous dream where the doorway opened out into empty yet luminous space. In this dream painting there is both a window and a door, two unencumbered openings onto the golden, clear light of the desert. In the painting Susan makes, the two uneaten pears sit in the window with an air of anticipation — a pregnant promise.

*A man tries to grab my purse; I fight him off, but he punctures my throat. No one will help me. I walk to my apartment holding cloths over my throat. Other girls are there. Women doctors and healers come to care for me.*

## "Silenced Voice"
### SEPTEMBER 29, 1988

SUSAN

*The attacker tries to take two things of value from me — my purse and my voice. When I fight for my purse, he punctures my throat. The taxi driver will not take me to the hospital; he doesn't want to get involved. I lie on the bed in my apartment holding cloths over my throat. The women come to my assistance, my doctor and some healers.*

*In this dream I am an adult, but when I make the painting of myself, I become a child. I know that this dream is about my silenced child's voice — so painful to lose, so difficult to reclaim.*

*At this time I have recently broken silence with my family. In a very painful revelation, I told them all I remembered about being sexually abused by Grandfather. I felt like a terrified child who couldn't imagine saying the words. My body felt big, dark, and empty. Inside was a child who was terrified of it really being real, terrified of being alone, and fearful of being denied.*

*In preparation for this speech, Patricia and I work to help me regain my power. I need to view myself as a courageous mother to my child, as an angry, protective adult. In the end, it is my artist-self who speaks for me. I use all my books of drawings and paintings to help me tell my truth.*

*My family is shocked and grieved by my story. They are angry with Grandfather and compassionate toward me. It is the best outcome that I could have hoped for. I tell my story because I have come to a point where I feel compelled to. I don't want to, but I really need to. The most important thing about telling is that I believe myself, because there are some people who are not receptive to the truth. I found that to be the case with Grandmother. At first, she seemed to be understanding, and then she became hardened in her denial and rejected me. I would not let her shut me out, and she eventually accepted me as I am — a granddaughter who stands up for herself. Later, I learned through a family relation that a cousin of mine acknowledged a similar experience with Grandfather. My cousin confirmed this with me, although we never discussed our details. However, I was told later that when my cousin was questioned by Grandmother, she denied everything.*

*I am learning that each time I share my story, though it is exceedingly difficult, I gain personal power and self-confidence. I know this telling has restored the power of my voice, and I don't hesitate to use it!*

## PATRICIA

One of the most important events in confronting the experience of sexual abuse is finding and using one's voice. Finding the memories, and believing in them enough to give them voice, is a major task in healing the traumatic aftereffects. Along with finding one's voice comes the necessity to break the silence by speaking the truth to others. For Susan this meant telling her family. This dream graphically illustrates the double-pronged wound of abuse. Not only is the purse, that premier image of precious feminine identity, stolen, but also the throat, the primary means of verbal communication, is punctured and rendered ineffectual. As the dream shows, the forces opposing speaking out against abuse are strong and vicious, and the taxi driver, the average "man on the street," does not care or want to hear or help. This dream moves into the collective arena as the dreamer finds herself with others who have been similarly wounded — "other girls are there." The need for help and healing from abuse is not merely a personal need but a cultural one as well.

*I am in the Caribbean looking for some jewelry made of coral. The woman shows me a trunk full of African turbans. She puts a black and jade green one on me. The cashier says, "I bought those only for Sophie."*

# "One Who Sees"

## OCTOBER 3, 1988

### S U S A N

*From this dream I make a painting of the woman who wears the black and green turban. She is dark and larger than life. The moon is backlighting her; stars surround her. I know she is the powerful guardian of the night, seeing all. I have come to feel her presence in a sense of personal security and self-awareness. I am no longer my own worst enemy, putting myself at risk. I have a new sense of observation, awareness, and self-confidence. When I look up the definition of "sophie, sophia," the dictionary says that it comes from the Greek word meaning wisdom and knowledge.*

### P A T R I C I A

For Susan the Caribbean is the homeland of the "One Who Sees." In the dream she is looking for some jewelry made of coral. This is not a search for lost jewelry as in a previous dream. This is a search for something new. Susan associates coral with gems from the deep seas.

I research coral and find that throughout the Mediterranean countries, coral is greatly valued, particularly as a magical necklace for children. It is supposed to protect the child from the evil eye. Coral is also referred to as the ocean's "tree of life," and its red color has mythic connections with life-giving female blood.

In her dream quest for coral, Susan is shown something different — a trunk full of African turbans. This takes us back to other dreams where Susan is given some kind of ritual garment to wear. Now, she receives a turban of black and jade. As a headdress, the turban wraps around the head holding and containing what is in the mind. She is told by the cashier that these turbans are only for "Sophie." When Susan looks up the meaning of "Sophie," she understands that the dream is about receiving feminine wisdom or knowledge.

In the painting Susan makes of the wise woman/moon goddess, she becomes one of the tribal woman initiators. She is the one who sees all with equanimity, and her seeing helps Susan to see, while the turban helps her keep her wisdom contained and held.

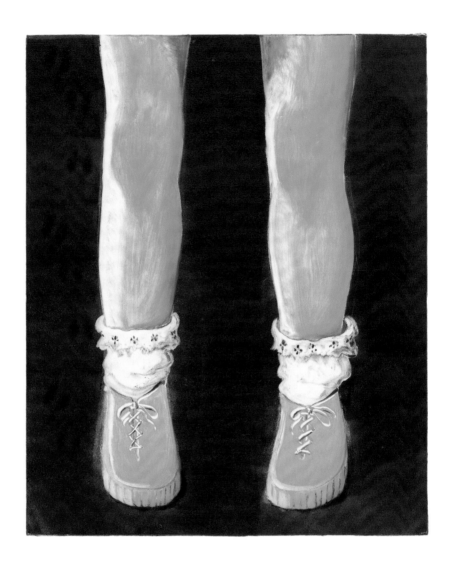

*I am in a Vietnam veterans posttraumatic stress disorder meeting. A friend has an instant flashback, like tripping and flipping out. He can't handle it. I am flashing back, too. I see my legs, small and thin. I am hanging. I know I am being tortured. The pain of this realization is excruciating. I am screaming and screaming. When I come back to consciousness, my friends are there, and they are crying. The therapist will have the police check two times to see if everything is all right. The flashback experience is intense and overwhelming, and I am afraid.*

# "Torture"

OCTOBER 4, 1988

### SUSAN

*I don't know what specific event causes me to dream this dream, feel this extreme pain. In the painting, my legs are small and thin, with baby shoes and socks. An unnamed torture has occurred. The feeling of accepting that reality is excruciating. It causes me to black out in the dream. In my recovery process, I have been going to that place of blackness to retrieve what it is I need to know. I can barely look at this painting even now.*

### PATRICIA

This dream comes the very next day after "One Who Sees." We are familiar with the dreams' by now predictable rhythm — a dream from the realm of initiation that includes the gift of powers, followed by a dream from the level of trauma. This dream's purpose seems to be to give us a full jolt of feeling reality, a visceral sense of what has happened to Susan. The graphic scene conveys the depths of what the abuse must have felt like to her child-self. This dream carries with it a tremendous emotional charge — so much that the dreamer blacks out, a protective response to too much pain, too much suffering, too much knowledge. When she comes back to consciousness in the dream, her friends are there crying.

It is very important that she sees and feels this response to her egregious injury. It furthers the healing process to know that others, especially friends, are emotionally responsive to what has happened. It cuts through the feelings of isolation and helps make things real. The detail of the therapist asking the police to check twice to see if everything is all right expresses a need for absolute surety and security.

This dream and the painting, done months later, are constant reminders of the depths of suffering and torture that the child-self endured.

$G$angsters are after us. They pull ahead in their car. I point a revolver out the window and shoot the center man. The bullet goes through the back of the head and out his eye. I feel no remorse.

# "Revenge of the Warrior Child"

## OCTOBER 29, 1988

### SUSAN

*This is an execution. I am not sorry. Once again, the dream shows me as an adult, but when I paint the image of myself, I become a young child. I am saddened because my task is not a child's task, and my expression is hardened and old. I made the warrior child red, to hold her anger and power, and I make Grandfather a revolting green. Plenty of blood was applied to be sure he is dead. In the previous dream, Grandfather got a thrashing. Now, he has been finished off. I am taking no prisoners.*

### PATRICIA

Because the grandfather is dead in waking life, Susan has to extract retribution and justice in the dream world. Although many would counsel forgiveness, it is important to allow for the full range of feelings, especially including revenge. Since no one in waking life was able to come to her rescue as a child, these events now happen in the dream world.

While making the painting, Susan recognizes that this kind of ruthlessness is a burden on the child-self, making her feel hardened and old. There is a price to pay for this much vengeance, this much focused rage. It is necessary but costly to be so merciless in her need to end the abuser's existence. This murderous revenge is aimed at the part of the grandfather that was sick and evil, the part that needs to be destroyed.

$A$ desert man who is my husband gives me a gift of loops of freshwater pearls and diamonds. His name is Hebeeb. He lives in a tent as a nomad.

# "Desert Man and Woman"

### DECEMBER 10, 1988

## SUSAN

*Freshwater pearls in the desert would certainly be a rare and valuable gift. The context of this dream tells me that the jewels are the gift of intimacy. The previous desert man offered me pears and presented the dilemma between emotional intimacy and physical distance. Here, the feeling is one of wholeness, and the valuable gift is given in honor of my sense of integration. It is the wholeness that comes from rejoining my fractured parts through the processes of remembering, suffering, and healing.*

## PATRICIA

This dream brought with it feelings of deep healing and gifts, fulfilling the promise of the pears in the earlier desert man dream. Freshwater pearls from the desert are the gift of great price.

Susan's realization that this gift of pearls is associated with sexual intimacy and wholeness is corroborated at the mythic level. I tell her that pearls are sacred to Aphrodite, the goddess of sexual love. Aphrodite's "pearly gate" is the entrance to her sacred vulva, so the gift of pearls, the "Pearls of Wisdom," represents complete sexual fulfillment — the masculine and the feminine consciousness are joined in perfect knowledge of the Goddess. The dream puts in an additional element, diamonds, to go with the pearls creating an even stronger image of the perfection of the Self. The painting that Susan makes from this dream shows the intimate moment of meeting.

*I buy a small box of berries and little fruits. On the way home, a big bird comes to eat them. He lands on the ground and gets bigger. There is a small boy inside the bird. He eats my berries.*

# "Big Bird Shaman"
## JANUARY 11, 1989

### SUSAN

*The bird was startling. Not only did it grow in size, but it also had a boy inside it. I gave my food to the great bird/boy. This is clearly a supernatural bird, the kind one finds in fairy tales. I don't know why the boy was inside. It is a mystery to me.*

### PATRICIA

This dream is indeed mysterious. It recalls the dream of "Thunderbirds," with the large, impressive archetypal birds and the small, "regular" birds that landed on Susan's upturned palms. This bird from the shamanic realm is a soul-carrier. It brings with it something human, a small boy. Is this dream part of the soul retrieval process? We know something is being brought to earth by the bird. And Susan's dreamer is feeding it from her own stores; she is beginning to give something back to the spirits that have helped her.

$A$ huge bear comes from the woods. The men have baited it with scent. The bear comes through the bushes, grabs the hunter with her claws, and wounds him deeply on the arms and chest.

# "Great Protector Bear"

## MARCH 4, 1989

### SUSAN

*This bear was the prey, then becomes the predator. The tables are turned on the hunter. This is a warning to those who would stalk, beware of the Great Bear Protector. I call upon this Great Bear for assistance and courage in difficult circumstances. The painting does in fact resemble my trusty German shepherd.*

### PATRICIA

In this dream the predator/prey relationship, which is a paradigm for childhood sexual abuse trauma, is turned around. The reversal shows that predator and prey exist together in the same drama. The bear, once prey, becomes predator, the hunter, once predator, becomes prey. When it comes to protection, the bear that is usually invoked is female. Susan's dreams seem to be drawing heavily upon the powers of the animal spirits for protection. I tell her that in ancient Greece the bearskin was worn by young girls who were dedicated to Artemis. The girls were called "little bears," and the bearskins were thought to protect them from early sexual involvement.

I feel from this dream that Susan is getting her teeth and claws back. She is in touch with her own deep instinctual ability to protect herself.

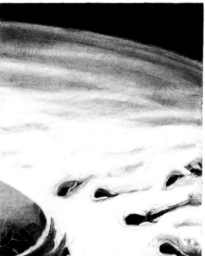

*I* take our little cow home on the bus; my sister comes along. I turn the cow out into the muddy field. On the hill is a Hopi clown dancer painted in red and white with feathers. As I ride by the pond, the waters move, and a great turtle climbs up from the muddy water. Polliwogs electrify the surface. It is spring.

# "First Turtle"

## SUSAN

*I take this dream and its feeling as a promise that life returns from out of the muck, like the turtle in spring. The electrified polliwogs are also a sign of regenerated life. Our little cow is fresh and young and is turned loose. Her companion in the field is the Hopi clown dancer, also known as a trickster and creator. His presence feels like a ritual rebirth. I am ready for some new life.*

## PATRICIA

The little cow is being brought home. The domesticated cow is a source of nourishment. She is being freed, given open pasture. In Hopi myth the clown dancer is the creator, and in one of the oldest and most durable Native American myths, the world is supported on the back of the turtle. The emergence of this turtle out of the primal waters indicates to us that a new world has arisen. The polliwogs are also a sign of spring. This dream occurs as an early harbinger of spring, the time of new life, new beginnings.

The dreams are changing in content and feeling. They are bringing an influx of creaturely energy. The "Bird Shaman" comes in from the sky-world; the "Great Protector Bear" comes out of the woods; the little cow is set free to pasture; and the "First Turtle" emerges from the spring pond.

151

*I am at the fairgrounds walking my beautiful horse. A Gypsy woman asks me if my beautiful horse is thirsty and gives him a drink of water, while a Gypsy man begins to harness his legs. "We need him for the race," he says. "Let him go; I don't race him," I say. We walk away.*

# "Wind Horse"

## SUSAN

*As I develop the painting of this horse, I try in many ways to show him with a human figure. The only image that works is to show him as a wild horse, alone and free, with a great wind in his hair. My wild horse energy is finally being loosed from the stall. All the little cows and horses are free to go. My body and spirit feel expanded and untethered.*

## PATRICIA

In this dream Susan is in a very different relationship with the horse than in the earlier dreams. The meeting with the Gypsies is a test. There will always be times when a trickster spirit will want to misuse her energy. But now, Susan is clear about the value and nature of her energy. She knows the horse is not to be used for profit or gain or any other kind of performance.

The horse that appears in the painting is wild, will not be tamed. But Susan, the artist, has a relationship with it. She honors the horse's need for an open range and will let the horse energy be free.

Susan titled the painting, "Wind Horse." This is also the name used by Tibetans for prayer flags that are placed outside in sacred places, mountain passes, near monasteries and homes. The "Wind Horse" as a central image, symbolizes upliftedness and confidence. The prayers on the flags fly out in the wind, carrying the messages of the Buddha and good fortune to all beings.

*A* very *large fish is in the water. He is hungry, and I give him pieces of fish from my mouth.*

# "Golden Carp"

MARCH 25, 1989

## SUSAN

*This dream evokes an ancient ritual of feeding the spirits. I know that indigenous peoples make offerings to the spirits in thanks for gifts given to the people. Here, I am feeding the fish from my mouth. This act marks a transformation of what has been held in my mouth. I am now producing something of value, a nutritious offering to my spirit fish.*

## PATRICIA

This dream is a counterpart to the "Purple Hearts" dream, where what came from Susan's mouth was indigestible bits of her trauma. Now a good and nourishing gift of food for the carp comes from her mouth. Again, there is the theme of feeding the creature spirits. I remind Susan that the golden carp is known for its longevity and is a symbol of good fortune in both Japan and China. Because it is a fish that swims against the current, it also represents courage and perseverance.

# "Abundance"

MARCH 20,1989

## SUSAN

*"Abundance" is an image that I made to represent the culmination of my self-recovery work. To create her I painted a woman who combines the characteristics of my many dream women. I painted her with rich honey-colored skin and deep soft hair. To celebrate her, I surrounded her with a wreath of red and white flowers. When it was time to print her image, I went to the print shop and found it closed for the holidays. I was distraught. I had no choice but to wrap her in plastic, which I knew could possibly destroy the image. The next day, I drove through deep mountain mud to another print shop where I uncovered her and found she needed extensive re-working. Through the re-working process, she became even more enriched and complex. My experience with this artwork became a perfect metaphor for the dreaming recovery process.*

# The Artist's Process

### SUSAN SNOW

Over a period of two and a half years, during my psychotherapy work with Patricia, I wrote down my dreams every day. Sometimes I would wake up and write in the middle of the night. Other times I would write in the morning. The more insistent dreams would pull me from a sound sleep demanding to be written down.

Only once did I feel compelled to draw a picture in the night; I wanted to capture the face I saw with the lipless grimace and the teeth (page 62). The image of the face compelled me with its fearful sense of recognition. This was the person who had hurt me; this time I would tell someone. After writing the dream down and making the sketch, I went back to sleep. The next morning I drew the entire dream sequence. Each important event became a drawing with captions for that particular moment; the dream was rendered as a story board. This is the method I used to record and preserve my dreams.

Each week, when I met with Patricia, we would choose a dream to discuss. Often, I would have drawn three or four dreams, sometimes with several drawings for each dream. While leafing through the drawings of the week, she would stop and ask me questions. "Who is this? What is going on here? What does this person signify to you?" Or, I would have a dream that I would want to discuss because it stood out from the rest as disturbing, or especially important to me.

There were also sneaky dreams, dreams that seemed inconsequential or unrelated to me. For instance, "Black Hole" *(page 26)*, where the drink was given to the child for pain, seemed to be about other people when I dreamed and drew it. It was a dream about a friend in therapy for depression who had discovered incest in her childhood. While Patricia and I were looking at the drawing, I had a strange sensation of being pulled down into a black void. I felt dizzy with recognition. The child in the dream was me; the mother was me; the mother was also my mother; and we were all linked to the experience of childhood incest. It was a stunning discovery that I felt in my body. Yet when I tried to stay emotionally connected with the dream image and gather more information, the connection just as suddenly left me. And so it went over a long period of time — my dreaming unconscious releasing bits and pieces of information to my conscious mind.

During my work with Patricia, I generated a large collection of paintings from my twelve notebooks of dream drawings. Aside from the first ten paintings in this book, all the rest of the dreamwork paintings were created in a very private studio space at an artist's colony where I would go for one month each year. I would bring all of my drawing books to work from, as well as new ones to fill. Sometimes I would search through the pages of drawings to find one that resonated for that day. Or I would make a list of important dreams and select one at a time to work with. Each day was different. Working with the dreams in this way prompted new dreams, creating even more material to work with.

Certain painful dreams I approached with dread. But I knew they were a part of the whole process, and I needed to paint them. "Purple Hearts" (page 100) is an example. There, I made a conscious choice to use ghastly colors to express the terrible sickness I felt when spewing up the objects of disgust. It was a purging process for me, a release of a long-held debilitating memory. While making the picture, I allowed myself to feel everything the dream was about, to cry, wail and whimper, be ill about it, and then let go of it.

Other dream paintings arrived in a different, more malleable process where the image was transformed through the process of creation. "The Combing" *(page 66)* is an example. The drawings from this dream were of me having my hair arranged by a maternal woman who was a friend. The dream described an everyday event in my kitchen, at my sink, with someone I knew. When I began the painting, I had to make choices about what colors I would use and how I would portray the women. I decided to strip the dream down to its sparest elements. I chose to simplify the figures by rendering them with one color — black — for its graphic richness. Then I put them in a universal kind of space where they became eternal, their actions timeless. During the art-making and decision-making process, the women were transformed from the ordinary to the archetypal or mythological realm.

Another process of change during the evolution of my art-making was the perception of an alternative sense of time. An example of this is "Grief" *(page 82)*. The dream and accompanying drawings were about a child's grief — wailing, drooling, and foreboding. When I laid on the paint to describe this moment, the drooling girl with the wavy hair became an adult me. She was no longer five, but thirty-five. This was not a conscious choice or a decision I made. I felt all the terror, sadness, and anxiety of this moment on a continuum from past to present.

After each of my marathon months of art-making, Patricia and I would meet and discuss all the paintings and drawings made during my time away. We had previously delved into and investigated some of the dreams. Others were new, spawned during the month-long art-making sessions. I was able to wade through a tremendous amount of material working this way.

A lot of processing occurred through the making of art — feeling, purging, releasing, integrating. Each painting had a resonance and meaning for me and helped me to more fully know and understand my story. This deep immersion in the creative process cut directly to the core of my issues, and gave me the opportunity, with Patricia's help, to make lifelong resolutions.

# The Dreamwork Teachings

PATRICIA REIS

The neurologist and writer Oliver Sacks has noted that, "It is the great discontinuities in life that we seek to bridge, or reconcile, or integrate, by recollection and, beyond this, by myth and art." He goes on to say, "All of us, finally, are exiles from the past." The dreams and art in this book demonstrate an urgent necessity in the dreamer to return to the past — to remember, recollect, and reunite the broken parts — through the creative process. Susan's dreams, art-making, and our mutual collaboration helped Susan bridge the void, the great discontinuity created by the traumatic events of her childhood. The dreams enabled Susan to feel and reconnect with deep emotions, physical sensations and realities, and to gain a sense of spiritual wholeness. The art became the bridge, Susan's way to journey into the unconscious and return with images, her soul no longer in exile from the past.

This remarkable process taught us much. In our exploration along the dreaming way, four particular teachings were gradually revealed through the two years of dreaming. First, the dream world generates its complex of images sequentially over many, many nights of dreaming. Second, the dream world remembers and brings information and responses from many co-existing realms. Third, creating visual art from dreams honors the dream world and renders the dream content in an especially powerful manner. Fourth, we can trust the dream's intent to show the healing way.

Although it is possible to gain significant meaning from a single dream, following dreams over a period of time, especially during critical times in one's life, yields richer, far more complex and complete information. As is evident from the sequence of dreams presented, Susan's dreams demonstrated a distinctive rhythm and pace. It was important for us to remember that when energizing, encouraging dreams came, they were often followed by painful, wrenching revelations. And vice versa. We learned to trust that agonizing dreams were frequently followed by celebratory ones.

The dreams often played off each other like sound and echo or variation and theme as they picked up an early image and added to it, and sometimes transformed it. For instance, the restless energy of the stalled horses in "Horse Sense" (*page 24*) became the working horsepower that pulled the dream barge in "Crossing" (*page 86*) and was later set free as "Wind Horse" (*page 152*).

The dreams' rhythm also related to the different co-existing dream realms — personal, archetypal, tribal, and shamanic. A dream bringing explicit information from the personal realm of abuse history, "Grief" (*page 82*), is followed by tribal women celebrating at Bloomingdale's (*page 84*). "Purple Hearts" (*page 100*) from the personal trauma realm is followed by one from the archetypal or mythical realm in "Scarlett O'Hara Meets Scarlett O'Hara" (*page 102*). The archetypal "Ariadne" (*page 42*) is followed by a dream from the realm of shamanic healing, "Shaman and Sputnik" (*page 44*). Together, we learned that although the dream world and its realms seem to operate independently and autonomously, they are all very responsive to the psyche's inquisitiveness and the artist's desire to engage.

As Susan explains her art-making process, we can see how creating visual art from dreams works to "dream the dream onward." The dream becomes amplified, enlarged, and further filled out. The drawings bring certain things to light; putting things on the table or the pedestal focuses our awareness. The painting process adds depth and dimension and the possibility of transformation. The ordinary becomes extraordinary. Meaning is enhanced, and significance becomes visible.

Finally, it was made clear to us time and again that the dreams' intention was toward healing on all levels. Reflecting on this process, Susan says, "I learned to honor and trust myself and my feelings and to function on a more whole, intuitive level. Through our work together, I experienced countless revelations that have promoted a sense of self-discovery and renewed self-worth. As an artist I have learned to value dreams as a fertile creative ground where my images are sown and reaped. Making visual art from my dreams continues to be my creative path."

As witness, guide, and companion in this process, certain things were demanded of me: a steadiness; a willingness to encounter the unknown; and a firm belief in the dream world's self-correcting and healing intention. Throughout our work together, I was frequently challenged by the feeling of unknowing, by the emotional anguish, by the mystery of what the dreams were showing. As a dreamworker, I was aware that very few people capture their dreams in such a coherent way, nor do dreams usually present with the clarity and precision that Susan's did.

Working on a sequence of dreams creates a relationship with the dream world that becomes increasingly revelatory. One reason we decided to produce this book is that the dreams' sequence had such definition and purpose we felt that it could be of use to others. I, myself, am now much more mindful of the possibility of pattern and integrity in individual dreams and in dreams over a period of time. Even if all I get is one hazy, fragmented piece of the puzzle, I can begin to make out, or intuit, a sense of the whole picture. This work has given me a certain familiarity with, and recognition of, some common themes that appear in other women's dreams, including my own. It has also given me feelings of deep respect and awe at the power of the dreaming way.

In my experience, it is unusual to have therapeutic work happen in such a condensed and concentrated way. Two and a half years is not a long time in therapeutic terms. When we began we had no idea of how long we would be working together. Once we were engaged, the work unfolded with an agenda of its own. Not unlike a birth process, the rhythm and timing were both happening to us and working with us. This was part of the third presence that we often felt operating.

Our mutual collaboration made this work possible. It was only by joining forces that we could both become students of the dreaming way. We chose to trust each other and the dreams' messages again and again as we followed the path of the dreaming way toward knowledge and recovery. We have each, in our own way, been deeply moved by the teachings of the dream world, humbled by its wisdom, and become ever more aware of the potential of dreams and their images to reveal and heal, or make whole.

I do not believe that one has to be an accomplished artist to achieve a fuller relationship with dream images. Nor does the therapist need to be specifically trained in art therapy or other techniques or modalities. All one needs is the willingness to engage dreams, some simple means of creating images, and an openness to the process. The strength of the therapeutic relationship is also important because the place where the dreams and images are shared, witnessed, and elaborated upon needs to be safe.

What makes this work unique is that Susan entered it with a great deal of artistic skill. The personal iconography of a dream becomes, in the hands of an artist like Susan, not only an emblem of individual recovery, but a gift to our collective memory. We are helped to remember not only personal history, but also the wisdom ways of healing. By reaching deeply into the dream, Susan, the artist, revitalized those images that had been lost to waking memory. Her work asks us to enter empathically with her into the realms of the dream world, to feel and intuit, to resonate and reflect on the images and their meanings. In this way, we as readers render something back to the dream source. As this work reminds us, we are all artists, poets, dreamers, born from Memory, the mother of the Muses, who comes to us with her healing visions in the night.

# A Conversation with Annie G. Rogers

*Annie G. Rogers is an Associate Professor in Human Development and Psychology at the Harvard Graduate School of Education. She is the author of* The Shining Affliction: A Story of Harm and Healing in Psychotherapy. *She is also a poet and painter. After reading the manuscript and seeing a presentation of our work, she wanted to talk with us about our relationship. One bright December morning in 1999, we met with Annie at her home near Cambridge. Sitting in her sun-filled living room around a small table, with tea and scones, we opened a conversation that gave us a chance to reflect on our work together.*

ANNIE: My first question is general, to set a context. Put simply, how did you come to work together?

SUSAN: I had been meeting with my physician at Women to Women, and she really encouraged me to see Patricia. (to Patricia) You had just arrived there.

PATRICIA: Yes, I had just started my practice at Women to Women. Dr. Christiane Northrup, who wrote *Women's Bodies, Women's Wisdom*, was the physician. She and three other women started this medical practice, and I leased office space from them in a renovated old house in Yarmouth, Maine. What was really great was that I was able to have a psychotherapy practice in the same house where women's bodies were being attended to. The practitioners there made referrals to me.

ANNIE: First sessions are often thought to be very important. How did it feel when you first met Patricia?

SUSAN: I felt comfortable from the very first few minutes. We would sit down on the floor, and she asked me to make drawings, usually drawings of my home and husband, drawings about my life.

ANNIE: Is this how you usually worked, Patricia?

PATRICIA: Well, I knew Susan was an artist and that she would probably work well visually. And during that first session, I probably asked you if you dreamed, if you remembered your dreams, and if you would consider drawing your dreams.

ANNIE: The dreamwork began right from the start?

PATRICIA: Yes, right from the start.

ANNIE: Were you in general working this way — sitting down on the floor, working with drawings and dreams?

PATRICIA: No, not all the time, not unless I felt that people would be responsive to working this way. But right from the start I really resonated with what your dreams were presenting and with how you were doing the drawings, Susan. Although it was often a work to open the dreams up, right away I went, "Oh ... "

ANNIE: Were you, "Oh," too, Susan?

SUSAN: The dreams were much clearer to me after I drew them, but while I was drawing them I didn't know *why* I was drawing them some of the time.

ANNIE: You had this initial session, or couple of sessions, and then right away you started to record your dreams?

PATRICIA: Yes. We established that way to work first thing. It is common for me to ask people to remember their dreams, but I had never come upon anyone, myself included, who had such depth of recall for dreams and ability to visualize them.

ANNIE: You went straight into that language, then? Susan, you seemed to find a process of your own that was extraordinary. How did this process ground you?

SUSAN: I was ready to go there and do that work. I had worked with some other therapists before, but it didn't work. With the idea that I could look at really deep issues, I said, "Yes, I can find my way around there." There were times when I wanted to quit. I would say, "Oh, maybe that's enough for now, or I don't have enough money, or I can't do this anymore." And Patricia would say, "Well, we can make the schedule work for you; we can trade artwork, but you can't stop working." I did try that a few times.

PATRICIA: I don't know if I wouldn't let you stop or if whatever was happening in the dreams was keeping us on task. The dreams entered as such a presence in the work that I felt, we can't stop this. So there was a feeling of this energy really pushing on us.

ANNIE: But you might have quit, given another therapist who wouldn't invite you to stay in this process?

SUSAN: I could feel Patricia's energy with me. She seemed to feel the things I was feeling.

ANNIE: How could you tell that?

SUSAN: Because she would say, "Ohhh, I felt that dark hole." Or after looking at a disturbing dream I would feel really dizzy, and she would say, "I felt dizzy, too." It was amazing to me that someone could be that empathic with what I was feeling. It validated what I was feeling and also put into words some of the feelings I would have — like this is a real feeling, a real thing that was happening.

ANNIE: How did a session usually go?

PATRICIA: We were meeting only once a week. When Susan came in, she would bring her big black sketchbooks, and we would sit on the floor and open them up. Those big sketchbooks were always in the mix; we were looking at them together.

ANNIE: So the dreams were like a third party?

PATRICIA: Yes. We would look at the sketches and try to open what was in front of us — what had been given to Susan — and it drew us in on all levels.

ANNIE: I am curious. During this time did Susan's dreams enter your dreams?

PATRICIA: This didn't enter my dream world per se; I don't remember Susan entering my dreams. But when we worked we were definitely in an energetic field together, and I was in there totally — no holding back. That's why Susan comments on my emotional reactions. I was trying to be as present as I could be. I tried to keep an openness — tried not being highly analytical or interpretive.

ANNIE: What about the interpretations that did happen?

SUSAN: Sometimes I would think a dream was about other people and their stories, and Patricia would ask me a lot of questions like, Who are these people? Where is that room? What are you feeling?

PATRICIA: Especially in the beginning as you entered the story. Sometimes there would be a physical sensation in your body, and then my body also. I would start to resonate with what was happening, so when Susan would feel dizzy, I would start to feel dizzy, too.

ANNIE: You would both feel dizzy?

SUSAN: Yes, and then all of a sudden it would stop.

PATRICIA: I would get dizzy, too. It was like vertigo, like being pulled into something. It was a strange sort of feeling. For me it felt like a deep pull from the unconscious. On the one hand, we were working in that very traditional hour a week format. That's how it was strung together in linear time. But I would feel the pull of the unconscious, and that was information for me.

ANNIE: One hour a week, one hour a week, one hour a week. How did all the hours in between, in which you were doing your own work, feel to you? Were you working on your own process?

SUSAN: I was dreaming, writing, and drawing.

PATRICIA: I think there was a certain safety in structuring the work that way. Sometimes there would be something mysterious in a particular dream, and then next week's dream would clarify. There was a storyboard way that Susan had of drawing, so we could begin to recognize a lot of the images. There were certain ways she would draw, and she didn't edit. She had a willingness to just put it out there. Sometimes in a drawing Susan would put something on a table and we would know, this is what is on the table.

SUSAN: Yes. I would make the drawing of the dream, and in the drawing there would be something on the countertop, sometimes with a light switched on near it. Like, Hello!! (laughter)

PATRICIA: It frequently felt like the dreams and the drawings were helping us. I am so often aware of the obscurity of dreams, but with your dreams, Susan, even if we didn't know right away what was shown, the dreams did not have that strange obscurity.

ANNIE: Did it feel that way to you, Susan?

SUSAN: In writing down the dreams, the meaning was sometimes obscure to me, but then I would make the drawing, and it was not so obscure. I would say, "Ohhh, that's my grandmother's house!" But it would be described in the dream like Motel 6 or something.

ANNIE: So you would write down the dream — I need to get a feel for this — you would write down the dream, and that would feel fairly obscure to you, in the sense that you didn't know exactly what the dream was telling you. Then you wouldn't think, "Well, I'll draw out this dream." You would just begin to draw or make something visual. And then what happened?

SUSAN: I would create the space that was described in the words of the dream. I would draw the picture, then I would recognize the content.

ANNIE: The drawing wasn't always what you set out to draw, necessarily?

SUSAN: Right. I would just draw out what I thought the dream had said. Then I would look at the drawing, and I could recognize that it was mine and see where it was from.

ANNIE: This is powerful in the way that it captures in a classical sense what are called the dream thoughts. The elaboration of the dream was actually built into your own process during the week.

SUSAN: Yes. I would spend several hours a week making drawings of my dreams. I eventually filled twelve large sketchbooks.

ANNIE: This may be hard to articulate. Did you feel that Patricia was with you during the week? (Susan nods) How did you carry her with you?

SUSAN: There were a lot of things she would tell me that I could take away and use — like how to interact with my family. As each thing would come up, I would have a reference back to something she had said.

PATRICIA: Yes. It was bringing that internal process into your daily life — so it wasn't just a circumscribed situation — like we were just in the dream world.

SUSAN: There were speaking dreams and wounded throat dreams, punishment and reward dreams for speaking out. All the different aspects of what could happen were shown in the dreams. I called upon my "speaking" dream character as an "outside of myself" person, although she was a part of me. I wanted her to talk for me. The dreams themselves are what I used the most in that process — the process of describing my childhood experience of incest.

PATRICIA: You finally did speak to your family.

ANNIE: You did it through the books of dreams and drawings?

SUSAN: I explained my experience through the drawings, with the pictures. I felt really small. It was really hard to do it, so I had to call on those big dream people to try to make it work.

ANNIE: What was it you were bringing to your family that allowed them to hear and know what to say back to you about what had happened?

SUSAN: My mother's responses were immediate. She did not look at the drawings with blank denial. She was compassionate, protective, and angry about what had happened to me.

ANNIE: How did you go on?

SUSAN: I don't think I had a choice. I couldn't go side-stepping; I couldn't go back. There was no other thing I could do.

PATRICIA: I think the dreams themselves helped. When the dreams delivered hard, really hard material, they would back it up with celebratory dreams. The dreams worked that way. They would prepare us by giving us a lot of energy, and then they would give us the really hard stuff, and then later we would get the reward. Also, I want to say that I trusted you from the first, that you were going to get into it and do it.

SUSAN: That wasn't obvious to me.

PATRICIA: Well, I felt there was a quality of integrity.

SUSAN: There was no pushing, no forcing.

PATRICIA: I think probably what we projected onto each other was helpful.

ANNIE: What about when you each ran into resistance, obstacles?

SUSAN: I remember only one time when Patricia said, "You are going to have to do this." (laughter) At first there was a certain topic I wanted to go around, that I really didn't want to address. I spent a long time avoiding it, probably months. I think she just got to the point where she said, "All right, honey, you are going to have to do this!" (lots of laughter)

PATRICIA: I don't actually remember that. But I can imagine it. (lots of laughter)

ANNIE: That's a very different way, though. After months of waiting, giving you plenty of time to observe yourself in this process, until you get tired of it, rather than pointing it out in a more energetic clinically pushy and/or negative kind of way — even the "honey" in it.

SUSAN: Yes. That's exactly what it felt like — a sister, aunt, or mother, someone like that, going "tsk." It's advice, giving advice. You didn't often tell me what to do, but that was the point where I was stuck.

PATRICIA: But I think what is unusual in a way is that whatever the transference/counter transference was, that wasn't where the actual work was happening.

ANNIE: No, it seems that you were open to one another, responded to one another, worked with one another in a way that I have always really said and thought therapy works best. When people do know what to do with one another, it creates a level of trust where the work can go really fast.

PATRICIA: I think that is definitely true, in the way that the work never went through a big period of dry spells, and the intensity was spaced out a little bit by the dreams themselves. We also had big influxes of support and energy from the dreams. Even when that big dream of all the pieces came smack in the middle — and maybe that's when you thought we were done (laughter) — and then it rolled out some more after that.

ANNIE: So, having all the pieces didn't mean having all the relationships between the pieces.

PATRICIA: No. But the dream that gave us that information was a huge support; like there was something to get here. And then you made that beautiful painting of the restored spirit bowl.

ANNIE: In the same way that you talked about physical responses of dizziness, terror, did you have bodily responses to these energizing, restorative dreams? I don't want to force that . . .

SUSAN: I was just thinking about that the other day, because I saw an image of a runner. After one of those really powerful healing dreams, I remember I was running at the time, and I felt a new, incredible lightness — a quickness, fast and free.

ANNIE: And when you sat with Susan and those kind of strengthening images appeared in the work, did you feel things physically too, Patricia?

PATRICIA: Yes, often there was a feeling like a whoosh of support — like those tribal women, anytime they showed up. I felt those images, and the animal images as well, lending just tremendous support.

SUSAN: Help is here; help is on its way. (laughter)

ANNIE: The question that goes through my mind, and it's hard to put into words, is how did you stay with the dreams for so long and trust them?

PATRICIA: I think because of the imagery and where it was coming from. And I had a deep respect for Susan's ability to stay with it.

SUSAN: I was in a deep service to the process. Everything was secondary, second to this. This work came first. And when it was done, because it was so exhausting, I let go of containing the dreams. I would continue to draw on that collection of dream iconography in my artwork.

ANNIE: Your art changed?

SUSAN: A lot! It changed a lot! I was a landscape painter; I did trees and rivers. Now I do crocodiles and sleeping women in burial mounds — all these wild things that I wouldn't have thought of.

ANNIE: It gave you access to a visual voice, a unique visual voice?

SUSAN: Those images are truly mine.

PATRICIA: There was also another thing going on under all this, because here we are now, and somehow we knew we had something in this work.

ANNIE: I was going to ask you about this. Where did you leave the relationship when you decided you were done?

SUSAN: I felt I had completed this body of work, but it felt great to have the door left open for me. I can reach out anytime and get counsel on any issue I may be struggling with.

ANNIE: There was no formal termination session at all?

SUSAN: No.

PATRICIA: What we knew was that there was a closing to the major piece of work that had lasted two years. Then after that, for about six months, there were some phone calls.

ANNIE: These were not regular sessions?

PATRICIA: No. Then there was the whole thing that happened six months later with the Institute for the Study of Dreams. They had a call for papers. At the time Susan had made slides of all her work, and this conference came up. I thought it was in Boston, but it was actually in London. I asked Susan, "Do you want to do this?" She said, "Sure." So we put together a sort of skeletal version of this book that we presented.

ANNIE: When you shifted from your week to week healing relationship to this other relationship, what was that like for each of you?

SUSAN: That was sort of scary. I had to be able to shift my way of relating to a more general, inclusive way — like eating lunch together or getting on an airplane.

PATRICIA: Before we went to London, I made a visit to your house, and you made a visit to my house. We talked about how to open up the container, because we had never met anywhere other than my office. Then it was, "OK, we are moving this out into the world now."

SUSAN: It was a little strange. I remember adjusting, trying to adjust, one little piece at a time.

PATRICIA: I think because what we had in that office space was so amazing in a way and so private, so contained.

ANNIE: Such a sacred and devoted time . . .

PATRICIA: Yes. And then there we were getting a room in London together, and I remember saying in the middle of the flight there, "Susan, if we get to London and you don't want to do any of this, it is fine with me." I felt very protective of you.

SUSAN: That was good. It was really the only way I could conceive of actually following though with the presentation.

ANNIE: Yes, I imagine that was crucial.

PATRICIA: I was still in that energy of being in service to the work, and I couldn't possibly do anything that I thought would harm Susan. And yet I also felt moved to present this.

SUSAN: I had never really thought about doing that. To me it was just the work I had done.

PATRICIA: It felt quite big to me.

ANNIE: Big in the sense you were able to think about other people trying to work with dreams, in the bigger world.

PATRICIA: Yes. Even though there is something quite unique in these dreams. Bringing this out took a lot of thought. Obviously, there is a power dynamic set up in a working relationship where someone comes, pays money, and expects an expert. We started to de-construct that form by going to each other's homes. All along I had a deep appreciation for Susan's creative abilities, as well as a deep respect for those other powers that were operating from the dream world.

SUSAN: There were many things I learned from Patricia, like appreciating the goddess, that taught me to value the feminine, to value myself.

ANNIE: And then you were traveling together to London. I would guess that first of all, if you'd had a complicated transference relationship, it would have been much trickier. Even so, it must have felt, particularly from your point of view, Susan, kind of strange.

SUSAN: I did find it strange, and it was actually before we left, or when we were on the plane, when Patricia said, "Even if right before we are going to get on the stage, you don't feel like doing this, you don't have to do it." And so I felt, OK, I can handle that. If I have the last minute choice to say, "No, I am not going to do that." It was the first time I had ever spoken the story in public. It was really overwhelming. But I hadn't really dwelled on it; instead, I focused on carrying the pictures, the artwork I had brought along. In the presentation itself, we showed the slides and spoke the dreams, followed by my comments and Patricia's comments.

ANNIE: Now here's a question for you. A lot of people in your shoes, Patricia, would have taken this material and presented it professionally as a "case." Why didn't you do that?

PATRICIA: I would never have done that, never, ever.

ANNIE: Why?

PATRICIA: This material belongs to Susan. It is your dreams, your artwork. I had no ownership. I had deep feelings about that. Either we presented it together, or it didn't happen.

ANNIE: It was clearly Susan's experience, Susan's artwork, Susan's story.

PATRICIA: Yes. Even though it came through in the context of our being together in this work. I did feel, however, that if it were made accessible to other people, it would be instructive, enlightening and enriching for them.

SUSAN: Through the process of speaking, I found I had a stronger voice afterwards, and then I just built on that. We presented the slide show a couple of times after that, and each time we presented it I had more to say.

PATRICIA: Even when we did this recently in Maine, I still felt a bit protective of you. I feel so strongly that whatever is done, we do it for growth, or health.

SUSAN: I do want to share the story in hopes that it will help other people; however, I've also learned how to protect myself. That's why I am choosing to tell my story here with a pseudonym.

PATRICIA: That also makes you trustworthy to me. You have that capacity for self-protection now.

ANNIE: As you are now, and as you look to the future, what is your relationship, and where is it going?

SUSAN and PATRICIA (simultaneously): We are friends.

ANNIE: So, you are "friends" in the truest sense. How extraordinary. Because so often it appears that a therapeutic relationship goes through a clear "termination" period, and then just ends. But here you have a mutually satisfying, deep friendship, yet what you did together was unmistakably therapeutic. What does it mean to each of you to be friends now?

SUSAN: For me it means participating in each other's lives. For example, some years ago I went on a Wilderness Dream Quest trip co-led by Patricia and Anne Dellenbaugh of Her Wild Song: Wilderness Trips for Women. And Patricia comes to my art openings and slide show talks with her friends. We also worked together on a major art exhibition about dreamwork. I curated the work, and Patricia wrote an essay for the catalog and participated in the panel discussion. Through our combined efforts, the show was very well received and created a lasting impact on the public. The things we do together as friends are always related to the creative and dreaming world. And I know I have someone who cares about what happens to me, and who is there for me when I call.

PATRICIA: Yes. I think that Susan and I have been very fortunate in that we have been able to build on our original collaboration. The qualities that helped us do the initial work together — trust, honesty, respect, a willingness to venture, and most importantly, our mutual passion for the creative process and dreams — provided the basis for all our further endeavors. Our partnership has translated well out of the therapeutic container and has been and continues to be a great source of enrichment and delight. As we branched out, we were also able to bring more of who we are as people to our relationship. We have different capabilities, skills, and competencies that are quite complementary. And there has always been, for me, another aspect — a sense of service to something bigger than our personal stories. That is where the true spirit of adventure and partnership lives.